VANISHING LADIES
and Other Magic

BY THE SAME AUTHOR

Norman Hunter's Book of Magic
The Incredible Adventures of Professor Branestawm
Professor Branestawm's Treasure Hunt
The Peculiar Triumph of Professor Branestawm
Professor Branestawm Up the Pole
Professor Branestawm's Great Revolution
Professor Branestawm Round the Bend
Professor Branestawm's Dictionary
Professor Branestawm's Compendium
Professor Branestawm's Do-It-Yourself Handbook
The Dribblesome Teapots and Other Incredible Stories
The Home-Made Dragon and Other Incredible Stories
The Frantic Phantom and Other Incredible Stories
Dust-up at the Royal Disco and Other Incredible Stories

Vanishing Ladies
and Other Magic
Norman Hunter

Illustrated by
JILL McDONALD

THE BODLEY HEAD
LONDON   SYDNEY
TORONTO

To the charming people in bookshops,
who conjure my books off the shelves
into the hands of readers

British Library Cataloguing
in Publication Data
Hunter, Norman
Vanishing ladies and other magic.
1. Conjuring – Juvenile literature
I. Title
793.8 GV1548
ISBN 0-370-30078-5

Text © Norman Hunter 1978
Illustrations © Jill McDonald 1978
Printed in Great Britain for
The Bodley Head Ltd
9 Bow Street, London WC2E 7AL
by Cox & Wyman Ltd, London, Fakenham
Set in VIP Baskerville
First published 1978

CONTENTS

Warning to Wizards, 7

VERY SIMPLE MAGIC
Mysterious Money, 13
Mystic Message, 14
It's a Gift, 16
The Bewitched Bracelet, 19
Clever Cards, 21
Birthday Magic, 22
Professor Branestawm's Spectacles, 23
The Disappearing Drink, 25
How to Un-press Flowers, 27
The Unripe Card, 29
Paper Surprise, 30
Escape from the Kidnappers, 32
Invisible Mending, 34
The Gairy Farland, 36
Jolly Jacks' Party, 37
Spots before your Eyes, 39
Weigh It and See, 41
It's Knot Magic, 42

MORE ADVANCED MAGIC
Follow my Leader, 47
The Ghost Writer, 51
The Great Crown Jewel Swop, 56
Sensational Vanishing Alarm Clock, 59
The Dieter, 63

The Wonderful Stick, 65
Double Colour-Changing Handkerchiefs, 68
Colourology, 71

MAGIC WITH PEOPLE

Magic with People, 77
The Girl from Nowhere, 82
Jill-in-the-Box, 84
The Vanishing Lady, 87
Quick Change, 89
The Haunted Tower, 92
The Magic Drum, 96
Sorcerer's Swiss Roll, 99
Down the Chimney, 101
Presents from Santa Claus, 104
The Great Escape Act, 106
On Guard, 110
Professor Flittersnoop and Mrs Branestawm, 113

Warning to Wizards

Dabbling in the magic arts, we are told, can be dangerous. But I promise you that you won't be carried off by coloured demons or consumed by frightful fire for practising the kind of magic described in this book. However, there is a sort of danger attached to it all the same. If you do one of these tricks badly it isn't likely to change you into a spotted dog. But it might make you look rather like a fool and I don't suppose you really want to look like that.

Fortunately there is a talisman to protect you against such misfortunes. It consists of a single magic word – 'practice'. You must practise these tricks, even the simplest ones, before showing them to an audience. That doesn't mean you have to spend fifty-six hours a day practising a trick. Just try it over a few times in private to make sure you can do it. This is important because, as I explained in my first book of magic, doing anything in front of an audience can be difficult. You're bound to be a bit nervous. Even tearing up a piece of paper can land you in difficulties if you haven't done it before with the kind of paper you're going to use. You may find the paper is so tough it won't tear, and then you're in bits instead of the paper.

But don't get discouraged and hurl this book into the waste paper basket. The great thing with magic, as with most other things except swimming, is to start at the bottom. By that I mean begin with easy tricks and go on to more advanced ones as you gain experience. It's much the same as learning to write, when you have to write out things like 'The cat sat on the mat,' before you can go on to such world-shaking statements as 'The chief product of North Snorton is burnt toast crusts and peanut porridge and the town stands on the south bank of the river Jolliwet and has a population of seven thousand, not counting the babies who will be born while this is being written.'

When you come to prepare a magic show, follow the same principle. Begin with an easy trick, one that you can do almost without thinking about it. Let it be a short trick and preferably with a surprise. The 'double colour-changing handkerchiefs' described in the 'More Advanced Magic' section is a good opening trick and very easy to do although you may find it a little difficult to make. Vary the tricks as much as you can, following the colour-changing handkerchiefs, for instance, with a card trick, then one with coins, and so on. But if you're going to do more than one trick with cards, do them all in a group; don't keep coming back to a card trick after you've done other tricks. Finish the performance with a showy trick in which you produce something pretty, such as 'The Gairy Farland' described in the first section of this book.

If you are able to get friends to help you with your show you would do very well to finish up with one of the pieces of 'Magic with People' described in the last section of this book. But do remember that if you are performing with other people who have to do secret things, you must rehearse the trick with them until you get it running smoothly.

Finally, when you have got a show together, don't change it. Keep on doing the same show over and over again. If you keep changing it and doing new tricks you'll always be nervous and never get the best out of the tricks. Of course, you won't want to do the same show to the same audience over and over again, but once you have a nice little magic show together you shouldn't have any difficulty in finding audiences. Old people's homes are usually very glad to have someone to entertain the residents and you'll find this kind of audience appreciative and sympathetic and this will give you confidence.

After you have done the same show a lot of times you will notice you can improve it with little changes here and there, by altering your tone of voice when you say something, or doing a trick more slowly or more quickly or making some other minor change. This will give you valuable experience and it's the quickest way to gaining a really professional manner. Then you can start making changes in the programme. Do this by taking out what you think is the weakest trick in the show and put in a different one. But don't change more than one trick. Go on doing the show over and over again before you make more changes.

If you think this sounds as if it makes magic rather boring for you, I can assure you that it will mean you aren't boring for your audience. And you can get a lot of fun trying over tricks in private to see which ones you like doing and perhaps even discovering different ways of doing them.

Now up with the curtain, if there is one but not if there isn't, and the best of good luck with your magic.

N.H.

Mysterious Money

You ask someone to take a number of coins and put them into a hat. 'Don't tell me how many coins you have put in the hat,' you say. 'In fact, don't tell me anything at all. But please note whether you have put an odd number or an even number of coins in the hat.'

You then say that, without asking any questions, you will add a few coins to the hat and make a magic change in them. If the number put in was odd you will make it even, and if the number was even you will make it odd.

You put a few more coins in the hat, and then ask the person who put the first coins in to say whether the number was odd or even.

You then ask someone to count the coins. And, sure enough, if the original number was even the number will now be odd, and if the original number was odd there will now be an even number of coins in the hat.

Ha! Very mysterious. All done by electronic mirrors and no end of invisible wires?

No. It isn't even done by hypnotism, thought transference, mind reading or indigestion.

HOW TO DO IT

It's so simple. All you do is add an odd number of coins to those in the hat. It doesn't matter how many coins you add as long as it is an odd number, three, five, seven and so on. Of course you could do the trick by adding just one coin to those in the hat, but this might give the show away. By adding, say, five coins you prevent the audience from comparing the original number of coins with the final number. If you just added one coin, the fact that the final number was just one more might lead people with very prickly brains to guess the secret.

Mystic Message

You take a sheet of newspaper and fold it several times. You tear pieces out, unfold it a bit and tear some more, then open the sheet and the audience see that you have torn out a message such as 'Happy Xmas' or 'Hullo!' or 'Ta-ta for now'.

HOW TO DO IT

Well, of course you don't really tear out the message because it's impossible, which is a very good reason for not doing it.

This is what you do. Take a sheet of newspaper, lay it flat on the table and with a soft pencil draw your message in nice, fat, block letters. Then, with a little skinny pair of scissors,

cut away the paper so as to leave the letters. Figure 1 shows you how to set it out. The dark parts are the ones you cut away. Make sure the top and bottom of each letter is joined to the paper.

Now fold this prepared sheet of newspaper into a packet a few centimetres square. Lay this packet on the corner of another sheet of newspaper as much like the first one as possible. Stick a piece of newspaper over the packet so that the folded newspaper is in a sort of little pocket on the corner of the other sheet. Have a look at Figure 2 which shows this.

To perform the magic, pick up the prepared sheet of newspaper, holding the corner with the packet in it in one hand so that your fingers hide the prepared part. Show the

paper both sides, then fold it several times. Tear out some pieces from the paper. While you are doing this you can say, 'You find funny things in the newspapers these days. People often get wrapped up in them. And look at the advertisements. Here's one that says, "Fatness is fatal. You can be fat free."'

Now unfold the paper a bit and tear some more pieces out. You can go on talking, saying that people use newspapers for various purposes, such as wrapping up things to keep the moth away, and folding up small to stop windows from rattling, and even for reading.

Go on tearing bits off the paper until you have torn all the paper away, including the patch, and this will leave you with only the prepared cut-out sheet.

Say, 'While I've been talking and tearing I hope you've followed me closely, because then you'll get the message ... Here it is.' As you say this, shake open the cut-out sheet and display the message which you have apparently torn out of the paper.

You can use the same cut-out sheet to do the trick over and over again. But not, of course, to the same audience because it has to be a surprise.

It's a Gift

You show a basin to be empty and pour some cornflakes into it from a packet.

'It's wonderful what free gifts you find in cornflakes nowadays,' you say. Then from the bowl of cornflakes you produce a number of silk handkerchiefs, some coloured ribbon and a small doll.

Ask Mum for an empty cornflake packet. Cut the bottom out neatly and then fix it about 5 cm from the top, inside the pack, with sticky tape. You now have a cornflake packet with the bottom quite near the top. Take some silk handkerchiefs and spread them out flat, one on top of the other. On them put a piece of ribbon, folded small, and a little doll. Fold the corners of the handkerchiefs into the centre to form a square package, then fold the corners of the package in to the centre again and put a clip over the corners to hold the bundle secure.

This bundle, which must not be too big to slip loosely into the cornflake packet, you put into the bottom part of the packet. Then put some cornflakes into the top of the packet. You now have what looks like an ordinary box of cornflakes but there are only a few cornflakes in the top of the packet and your bundle of gifts is in the bottomless lower part.

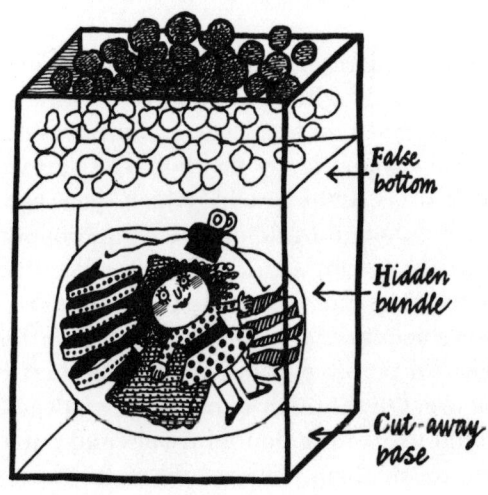

Come forward with a fairly large, deep basin in your left hand and the prepared cornflake packet in your right. Keep a finger of the right hand under the packet so that the bundle doesn't fall flomp on the floor and give the whole show away.

Show the basin to be empty and put it on the table. The sort of table to use is one of those little round ones with a skinny little top about the size of a dinner plate. You put the packet into the basin while you show the packet contains cornflakes. By using a very small table you have to stand the packet in the basin because there isn't room for it beside the basin. Very crafty. But if you can't find a skinny little table you could use a kitchen stool with a small tray on top of it, or, failing that, you can use whatever table you have and still put the packet into the bowl while you show the cornflakes, but the effect isn't quite so good.

Now, having trickled a few flakes through your fingers, lift the packet out of the bowl, when of course the bundle of gifts will stay behind in the bowl. The audience will still think the basin is empty because they don't know what you're going to do.

Pour the flakes from the packet into the basin. Say how amazing it is the gifts you find given away with cornflakes these days. Then undo the clip and produce the ribbons, silk handkerchiefs and lastly the doll. The kind of clip to use is one called a Bulldog clip which you can get from a stationer's, though Mum or Dad will probably have one. Or you can use a clothes peg. Silk handkerchiefs are rather expensive, but most shops that sell things like that have handkerchiefs and scarves of a sort of chiffon, which are cheaper. Or perhaps Mum may have a scarf or two she will let you use. On the other hand, if you can't get anything else you could use some coloured tissues and put a folded paper garland inside them. This would make a nice display when produced.

The Bewitched Bracelet

You show a bracelet and tell the audience it has magical qualities. 'It was given to one of the daughters of the King of Incrediblania,' you explain, 'by an old lady who came to the door, selling steering-wheel covers for motor-cars. They didn't have motor-cars in Incrediblania but the Princess bought one because she was sorry for the old lady. And of course the old lady was really a fairy and gave the Princess this bracelet for being kind.'

You hand the bracelet to the audience to look at and while they're inspecting it you get two people from the audience to tie a length of string or thin cord to your wrists, one end to each wrist.

Now you take back the bracelet and say you will show the magic powers it possesses. 'I'll just walk round this screen,' you say (if you don't have a screen you can just walk out of the door and back), 'and you'll see what the bracelet can do.'

You walk round the screen (or out of the door and back) and the audience see that the bracelet has threaded itself on the cord between your hands.

Cord and bracelet can be examined because the bracelet doesn't come apart or have any gaps in it, so the whole thing is nice and impossible.

HOW TO DO IT

The bracelet really doesn't open anywhere. It is plain and solid. But you'll need two bracelets exactly alike. Don't get bracelets costing a thousand pounds each because that will use up too much pocket money. Just get two plain metal or plastic bracelets exactly alike.

Before you show the trick, put one of the bracelets on your arm and push it right up under your sleeve until it grips tight on your arm.

Now, when the cord has been tied to your wrists, all you have to do is take the visible bracelet from the audience and, as you walk round the screen or out of the door and back, simply put the bracelet in your pocket and pull the hidden bracelet down your arm and on to the cord.

'There you are!' you say, as you reveal it threaded on the string. 'That's the magic power of the bracelet and it may not seem to be of much use but at least it's just as useful as a steering-wheel cover in a country that doesn't have motor-cars.'

Clever Cards

You ask someone to choose a card, look at it and then put it back into the pack.

'These cards are very clever,' you say. 'They help a magician to do his tricks. For instance, if I want to know which card you chose I just ask the cards to tell me, and they do.'

As you say this, you spread the cards out on the table, faces down, and the audience see that one card has turned itself over and is face up. This is the card that was chosen.

HOW TO DO IT

Train the cards on pancakes so they'll turn themselves over? No, no, much easier than that. When the card has been chosen you turn your back while the audience are shown the card, so that you don't know what it is. But really you turn your back so that you can secretly turn the pack over and turn the bottom card over. All this turning is a good turn for you because now you have the pack upside-down but it doesn't look like it because the card on top has its back upwards. Because the cards have white borders (most packs do but you must be sure to use this kind), it looks as if all the cards are back up but really only the top one is.

Have the chosen card pushed back into the pack. Of course it will be the opposite way round to the other cards but nobody knows.

Now all you have to do is secretly turn the pack over and spread them out on the table, when the chosen card will be seen to be the only one face up. Oh yes, I know; how about the card on the bottom of the pack that you turned over secretly at the beginning of the trick. This would be face up as well as the chosen card, wouldn't it? Well, you get over this little difficulty by dealing this card out on to the table face down first as you say, 'These cards are very clever'. Then you just spread the rest of the cards out. It seems a quite natural thing to do and nobody will suspect it has anything to do with the secret.

Birthday Magic

I'm afraid this doesn't enable you to produce lavish birthday presents out of thin air. But it's a good bit of magic. You begin by asking someone to write down the year of their birth and show it to you. You then write something secretly on another piece of paper, seal it in an envelope and ask them to put it in their pocket. Then you ask them to choose either the first two figures of the year of their birth or the second two, and then to pick one of those two figures. 'Now open the sealed envelope I gave you when we started,' you say. They find you have written on the paper in the envelope the very figure finally arrived at.

HOW TO DO IT

No computers or crystal balls needed. It's all done by what is called conjurer's choice. Suppose the year written down is 1968. You then write down the figure 6 on a piece of paper. Don't let anyone see what you've written; just seal the paper in an envelope.

Now, when you ask for either the first two or the last two figures of the number to be chosen, if they choose the first two you cross them out. If they choose the last two, say, 'That disposes of the others,' and cross out the first two just the same. This leaves you with the figures 6 and 8. Ask the person who wrote down the year to choose either figure. If he chooses the 6, ask him to open the envelope and he'll find you predicted the number he's chosen. If he chooses the figure 8, cross it out, as you did before, and ask him to open the sealed envelope when he'll find the figure left.

One small point. If the person you choose was born in a year with two figures the same, such as 1969, it is better to get someone else to write their birthday year because you want all the figures to be different.

Professor Branestawm's Spectacles

You tell the audience that Professor Branestawm wanted to read the newspaper but couldn't find his spectacles. So he put the newspaper on his breakfast plate while he went to look for them. In the meantime Mrs Flittersnoop poured cornflakes on the plate and when the Professor came back he found his missing spectacles among the cornflakes in the plate. He said it was better than finding plastic aeroplanes in the cornflakes.

HOW TO DO IT

You need a folded newspaper, a cornflakes plate and a pair of spectacles. Toy ones will do but it is even better to make a pair out of cardboard and paint them black. Put the spectacles under the back edge of the folded paper on your table and lay a plate on top. It must be a deep plate of the kind you use for breakfast cereals. While you are telling the audience about the Professor, pick up the folded newspaper with your right hand, holding the spectacles secretly underneath. Figure 1. Show the plate and put it upside-down on the news-

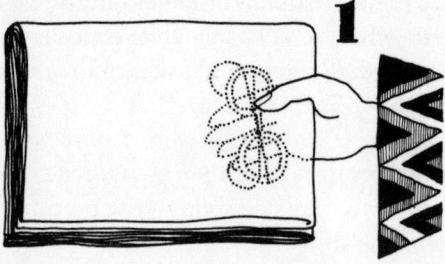

paper and hold it there with the thumb of your right hand. Now with your left hand draw the newspaper away. This will leave you holding the plate upside-down in your right hand, with the spectacles inside it. Figure 2. Turn the plate over and cover it with the newspaper, taking care that the audience don't catch a glimpse of the spectacles in the plate.

You don't need any cornflakes but if you like you can lift

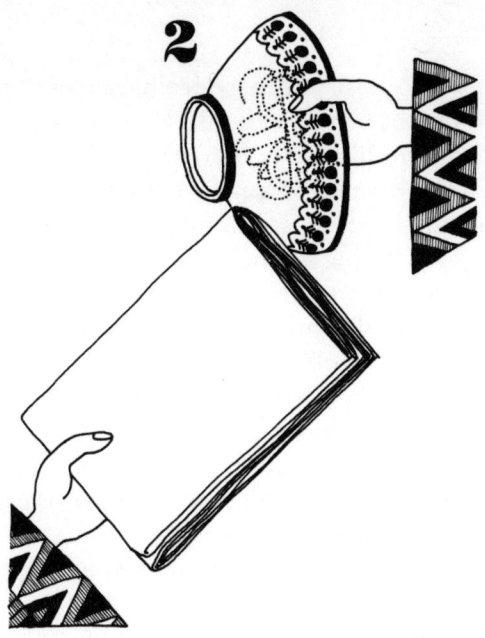

the back edge of the paper and pour some cornflakes over the spectacles. Spectacles made of cardboard are best because they don't make a sound when you get them under the plate.

The Disappearing Drink

You pour out a glass of water and cover it with a handkerchief. 'Making a drink disappear is easy,' you say. 'You just drink it. But magicians prefer to do it the hard way, like this.' You shake out the handkerchief and the glass of water has vanished.

HOW TO DO IT

For this you need a transparent plastic tumbler and a jug that has some pattern on it, such as a cut glass pattern or fluting. You also want two handkerchiefs, both alike, sewn together round the edges, with a disc of card the same size as the top of the tumbler sewn between them in the middle.

To perform the trick, pick up the tumbler in your left hand and the jug, full of water, in your right. Pour water into the tumbler and put the jug down. Now pick up the handkerchief and throw it over the tumbler. Let the tumbler slip into the jug and hold the disc of cardboard in the handkerchief, which will look as if you are holding the tumbler under the handkerchief. Figure 1. Move away from the jug and at the right moment flick the handkerchief in the air and the tumbler seems to vanish. The tumbler of water in the jug will be quite invisible because the cut or fluted pattern on the jug and water will completely camouflage it.

This is quite an easy trick to do but you must practise it a bit so that you can let the tumbler slide into the jug neatly and unnoticeably.

If you don't want to go to the trouble of sewing the cardboard disc between two handkerchiefs, you can use a large paper serviette or a sheet of newspaper. Mould this round the tumbler and let the tumbler slip into the jug as before.

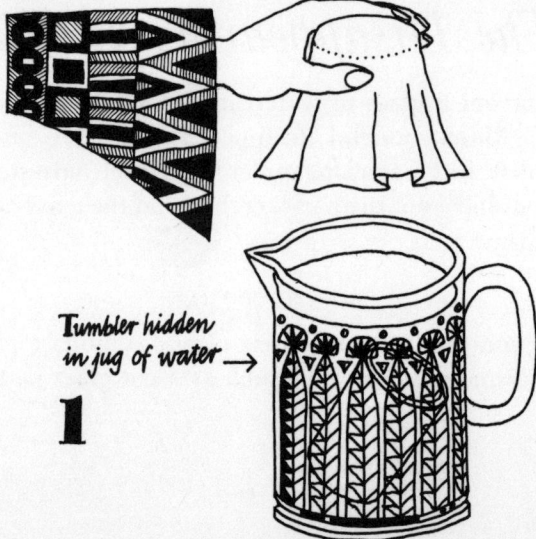

Tumbler hidden in jug of water →

1

How to Un-press Flowers

'Professor Branestawm thought pressing flowers was a bit silly because when you've squashed them flat, what use are they? So he invented a method of un-pressing pressed flowers.' As you say this, you pick up a book and thumb through a few pages. 'To press flowers you usually put them between the pages of a nice, fat, ferocious book, close the book and in due course the flowers are pressed flat, ready to stick on collages or throw in the dustbin.'

You show a couple of pieces of paper painted to look like flowers and say, 'These aren't really pressed flowers but they look as if they are. I'm going to put them into the book and un-press them by Professor Branestawm's method.'

You put the flat flowers between the pages of the book, close it, bang it on the table, open it again and take out two perfect, un-pressed, lovely three-dimensional flowers.

HOW TO DO IT

To do this you want an old book, a fairly thick one. Turn over about a quarter of the pages, then cut out the centres of the rest of the pages, making a hollow space in the book. Figure 1. Into this you put two flowers. Imitation ones made of plastic are the best as you can use them over and over again. Then you paint copies of these two flowers on paper and cut them out.

While you are talking about the Professor's idea, you pick up the book and flick over a few pages. These of course are the whole pages at the beginning of the book. Keep your

thumb on the part where the pages are cut out to stop them from moving.

Put your two flat paper flowers into the loose pages, close the book, bang it on the table, then open it at the cut-out part and take out the flowers.

If you find difficulty in controlling the cut-out pages you can stick them together with a dab or two of paste between the pages, but this isn't really necessary and the book looks more natural if you leave the pages loose.

Now perhaps Professor Branestawm will be kind enough to invent some chocolates that will re-appear after you've eaten them so that you can eat them again.

The Unripe Card

You show a playing card, the four of diamonds. 'Notice what nice red pips it has,' you say. 'That's because it's ripe. Sometimes you get an unripe card and then it looks like this.' As you say these words the pips of the card turn bright green.

HOW TO DO IT

For this you need a special card and this is how to make it.

Take a four of diamonds from the pack and carefully cut out the four pips. Figure 1. Mum or Dad may have a sharp knife such as a Stanley 99 and be willing to do this for you. Now take another card and cover the top half of the face with green gummed paper and the bottom half with red gummed paper as in Figure 2. You can buy packets of gummed paper squares in assorted colours at most stationers.

Next you need a piece of different card. This must be just over half as long as a full playing card and a tiny bit wider than a card. Cut it quite a bit wider to start with and you can trim it later. Cover the top half of this piece of card with red gummed paper and the bottom half with green paper. See Figure 3.

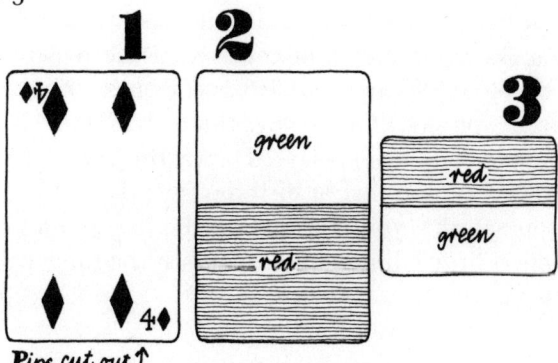

Stick the card with the cut out pips on top of the red and green card, but glue it only along the top and bottom, with a very thin line of glue. When the glue is quite dry, push the other piece of card in between the two stuck cards, with the colour side showing under the cut out pips. But see that the red half of the piece of card comes over the green half of the back card. The edges of this piece of card will project at the sides of the double card. Carefully trim them so that they project only a very tiny bit, just enough, in fact, for you to slide the piece up and down inside the double card by holding it at the sides.

To show the trick, hold up the card with the sliding piece arranged so that the pips all appear red. As you talk about cards being unripe, you slide the piece of card to the other end of the double card and the pips will all change to green.

Make up this trick card carefully and you'll find it works like magic.

Paper Surprise

This is a very pretty trick, and quite easy to do.

You show some pieces of coloured tissue paper. 'These pieces of coloured paper were left over from a Chinese birthday party,' you say. 'The strange thing about them is that, if you crumple them up and say, "Happy Birthday", they turn into a nice Chinese sort of birthday surprise.'

As you say this you crumple up the papers and change them into a little Chinese paper lantern the same colour as the papers.

HOW TO DO IT

You want one of those little Chinese lanterns that you can buy where they sell Christmas decorations. The lanterns are made like a concertina and fold down flat. To the outside of the bottom of the lantern stick a little loop of sticky tape because you'll want this to hold the lantern with later on.

Now take some pieces of coloured tissue paper, the same colours as the lantern or fairly near. The pieces should be about 12 or 15 cm square, but you may have to vary this according to the size of the lantern. Fold up the lantern and stick the middle of one piece of tissue paper to the bottom of the lantern, inside. Lay the other pieces on top and you are ready.

Pick up the papers, holding the lantern hidden behind them. Talk about the Chinese birthday party and as you crumple the papers, push them into the lantern with one hand and pull the lantern open with the other. The little loop of tape you stick to the bottom of the lantern will help you to do this.

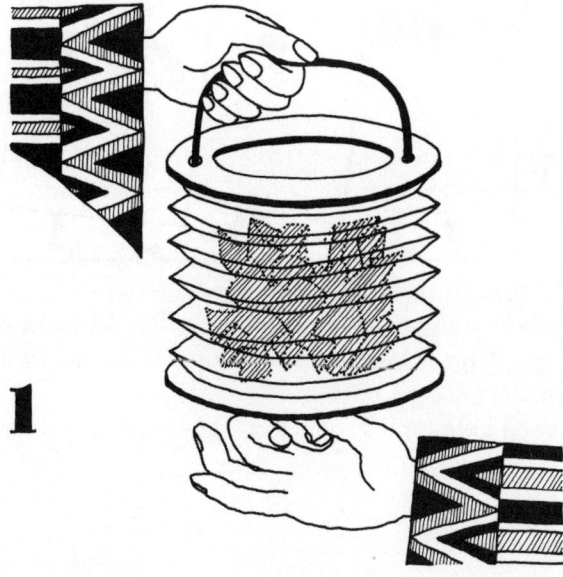

As the lantern opens it swallows the tissue paper and the papers seem to have turned into the lantern. See Figure 1.

It's best to find out by experiment what size papers you need because you want to make sure they're big enough to hide the lantern at the beginning of the trick but not too big for the lantern to swallow afterwards.

Of course you can't have a light in the lantern but you can explain that by saying you want to keep the audience in the dark about the secret.

Escape from the Kidnappers

Here's a topical piece of magic.

You show two red luggage labels and a white one. You thread them on a long piece of string with the white one between the two red ones.

'This is a kidnapping,' you say. 'The white label has been

kidnapped by the red ones and held to ransom for four and a half pence, two Professor Branestawm books and a wine gum. Will two people please come and act as police and hold the ends of the string. Don't bring your guns because the newspapers will make any necessary reports.'

You give the ends of the string to two people from the audience. Then you throw a handkerchief over the labels on the string.

'The kidnappers thought they were on to a good thing,' you say. 'But their victim had them on a piece of string, as you can see. Under cover of darkness he escaped.'

You show your hand to be empty, put it under the handkerchief and remove the white label intact and undamaged. Then you take the handkerchief off the string and the audience see the two red labels are still threaded on it but the white one is no longer there.

HOW TO DO IT

This is a puzzling trick, but very easy to do. All you need is an extra white label. If you can't get real luggage labels you can make them from coloured paper and punch a hole near one end to thread on the string.

To prepare for the trick, put the second white label in your pocket or on the table, under the edge of the handkerchief you are going to use. Show the two red labels and the white one and thread them on the string, pointing out that the white label, the kidnappers' victim, is between them and cannot get off the string because they are preventing him. Get two people to hold the ends of the string and stretch it tight. Now pick up the handkerchief and with it pick up secretly the second white label, folding it across the middle. Throw the handkerchief over the labels on the string and hang the second, folded, white label over the string too, where the handkerchief will keep it in place.

Show your hands to be empty, reach under the handkerchief and tear the white label off the string. Crumple it up in your hand. With your empty hand smooth out and show the second white label, and draw the handkerchief off the string with the hand concealing the torn label. Crumple the handkerchief with the torn label inside and put it aside. To make the trick even more effective you can draw a £ sign on the white label before you thread it on the string, having previously, of course, drawn a £ sign on the second white label.

Invisible Mending

You show a piece of ribbon about a couple of metres long. Then with a pair of scissors you cut several pieces out of the middle of it.

'Cutting ribbon is easy,' you say. 'But mending it so that the join doesn't show is impossible. That's why Professor Branestawm invented a way of doing it. All you do is rub the cut ends of the ribbon with the non-cutting end of the scissors.'

You rub the handles of the scissors on the ribbon, then draw out the ribbon and everyone can see it is completely restored with no sign of it ever having been cut.

HOW TO DO IT

The world-shattering secret of this bit of magic is that you didn't cut the ribbon in the first place. At least not the long piece of ribbon the audience think you cut.

To prepare for the trick take a short piece of ribbon, about

14 cm long, fold it and put it between the leaves of a book so that the looped centre sticks out a bit. Have the book on your table with the ribbon to the back where it isn't seen. Figure 1.

Show your long piece of ribbon, take it by the middle and lay it over the book so that the centre of the ribbon comes over the hidden piece. Show the scissors, put them down, then pick up the ribbon by the centre, picking up the small piece too, drawing it out from the pages of the book. Apparently draw the folded centre of the ribbon through your hand but really leave the ribbon concealed in your hand and draw out the loose piece. Figure 2.

Now cut the loose piece of ribbon, which the audience will think is the long piece. Cut it several times, finally cutting and pulling away all the short pieces of ribbon. This leaves you with only the long piece of ribbon in your hand and you can then draw this out and show that it has apparently been magically mended.

If you find ordinary ribbon is too expensive, you can do the trick just as well with the cheaper ribbon sold for tying up presents, or you could even cut some strips of white or coloured paper to use as ribbon. The short piece must, of course, be the same kind and colour of ribbon as the long piece.

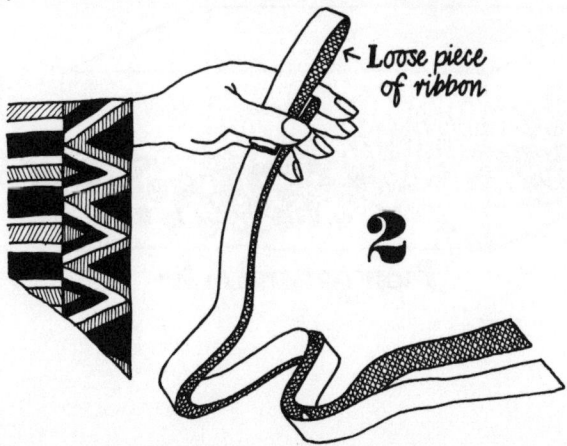

The Gairy Farland

You fill a small tin with confetti and say, 'The fairies will now stick all those bits of coloured paper together to make a Gairy Farland... er... no, I mean a Garly Fairland... no, no, a... oh, one of these.' You take from the tin a long paper garland, saying, 'That's it, Fairy Garland.' The confetti has all vanished.

HOW TO DO IT

You will need two tins that once contained tinned fruit or beans or something. Small tins, about 10 cm tall and 5 cm wide are best. Cover them with fancy paper, or paint them so that they both look alike. Then cover the bottom of one tin, on the outside, with a thin layer of glue and stick on lots of confetti. If you stand this tin upside down it will look as if it is a tin full of confetti. Get a small paper garland, put it inside the tin and lay the tin on its side in a cardboard box. A shoe box is about right. Pour some confetti into the box and put the empty tin beside it. Figure 1.

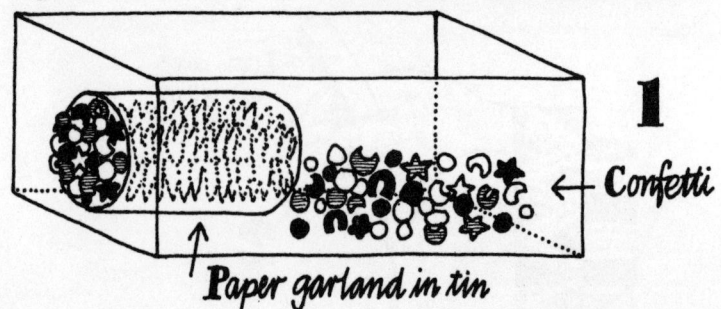

To perform the trick, show the unprepared tin to be empty and fill it with confetti by dipping it into the box and scooping the confetti into it. Pour the confetti back into the box and apparently fill the tin again. This time, however, you leave the empty tin in the box and bring up the fake one, keeping a finger across the bottom to stop the garland from falling out.

As you say you are going to ask the fairies to make a Gairy Farland out of the confetti, wave the tin in the air and turn it over. Or you can cover it with a large handkerchief and secretly turn it over under cover. Then you produce the garland and show that the tin is empty once more, but keep your hand over the bottom of the tin so that the audience cannot catch sight of the confetti covering the bottom.

You can, of course, use something other than confetti and turn it into something other than a garland. For instance, you could use sawdust and turn it into a solid block of wood, and then describe it as Professor Branestawm's invention for re-constituting sawdust back into wood again.

Jolly Jacks' Party

You show the four jacks from a pack of cards, put one at the bottom of the pack, two more in different parts of the pack and leave the fourth on top.

'These four jacks are now going to have a party,' you say.

'In fact, a get-together.' You put the pack on the table and cut the pack by lifting about half the cards off and putting the other half on top of them.

'By just cutting the pack like that,' you say, 'I've brought all four jacks together for their party.'

You spread the pack out faces upwards and the audience see that all four jacks are together in the middle of the pack.

HOW TO DO IT

All you need is a pack of cards. Just ordinary cards, not double-faced cards or automatic clockwork cards or highly ingenious folding cards. Take the four jacks from the pack, lay one face up on the table, put two kings on top of it and lay the other three jacks on top of them.

You do this secretly, of course, beforehand. Start the trick by showing the four jacks held out in a fan, keeping the two kings carefully hidden behind the front three jacks, as in Figure 1.

Now square up the cards and lay them on top of the pack. Pick up the top card, which is a jack, show it and put it on the bottom of the pack. 'This jack lives in the bottom flat,' you say.

Take the next card, which the audience think is a jack, but which is really a king. Don't show it, but put it somewhere in the lower part of the pack. 'Jack number two has apartments on the first floor,' you explain.

Now take the next card, which again the audience think is a jack but is really a king, and put this somewhere in the pack above the last card you put in. 'Jack three lives on the second floor,' you say.

Then show the next card, which *is* a jack, and put it back on top of the pack, explaining that this jack lives on the top floor.

'Now let's bring them together for a jolly jacks' party,' you say. Put the pack on the table, lift off about half the pack and put the other half on top.

If you now spread out the cards, faces upwards, you will see that all four jacks are together in the middle of the pack.

The idea of using kings for the extra two cards is that if someone should catch a glimpse of these cards they will look sufficiently like jacks not to give the secret away.

Spots before your Eyes

The spots are on a little dice, the kind of thing you use for throwing numbers when playing reckless games of ludo. You hold the dice between your finger and thumb and ask your audience to notice what number of spots is on the side facing them. Suppose it is four. 'Spots before the eyes can be very confusing,' you say. 'In fact you can never be quite sure how many spots there are.' You give your hand a shake and the audience see the four spots have changed to six.

Now you turn your hand over and show that there are

three spots on the underneath face of the dice. Then asking the audience to watch the dice very closely, you turn your hand back again and they see that the six spots they saw on the first face of the dice have changed back to four.

HOW TO DO IT

Ha, mechanical changing dice with electrically operated spots, invented by Professor Branestawm? No no, thank goodness! Just an ordinary little dice. You hold it between finger and thumb as shown in Figure 1. To make the spots change secretly roll the dice over as in Figure 2. You cover this move by a slight wave of the hand.

Now, when you turn your hand over to show the underside of the dice (Figure 3), you secretly roll the dice back. Then you have only to turn your hand slowly back to show that the spots on top of the dice have changed again. It's very easy. Just try it with a dice in your hand. And of course if you don't succeed at first, well, never say you know what.

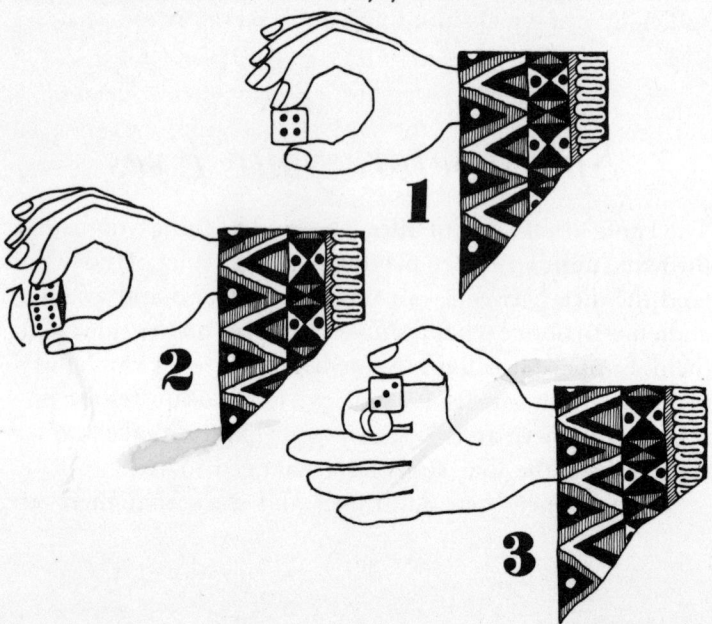

Weigh It and See

This is a card trick. But it's a kind of card trick you don't often see. No cards are chosen or anything like that. You show a pack of cards and get someone to shuffle the cards. Then you say, 'Most people don't know that cards with black pips are heavier than cards with red pips. Don't ask me why, but there it is. For instance, this first card is a heavy one, so it is black.' You turn over the top card and sure enough it is a black one. Then you go on weighing the cards one by one and saying whether they are red or black before turning them over. And you are right every time.

The pack can be shuffled as often as you like and it is a perfectly ordinary pack of cards, not a specially made one.

HOW TO DO IT

This very easy but effective piece of magic depends on using a pack of cards with what is called a one-way pattern on the back. That is to say, the pattern consists of a picture of flowers or something of the kind so that if you turn it upside-down it looks upside-down. Many packs of cards have an all-over pattern on the back that looks the same either way up but you will be able to find a pack with a one-way pattern quite easily.

Before the show, arrange the cards so that all the black cards have the backs one way and all the red cards have the backs the other way. Now shuffle the pack and you are ready.

Now you can tell by the way the pattern on the back faces whether a card is a red one or a black one. But you disguise this secret by pretending to weigh the cards. Only when you get someone to shuffle the cards, for goodness' sake do make sure they can shuffle a pack! It would be the most frightful awfulness if someone dropped the cards all over the floor while shuffling them because then you couldn't be sure of doing the trick.

It's Knot Magic

You throw two handkerchiefs in the air and they tie themselves together.

Easy as eating cream buns with a pair of pliers! Put the tips of your first and second fingers and thumb of your right hand together and slip a small elastic band over them. Show the two handkerchiefs. Put them both into your right hand, holding each by a corner, and let the elastic band snap round the corners. Now throw the handkerchiefs in the air and they'll appear to be tied together.

Now another knotty one, this time with six handkerchiefs, if the family have that many. You show three of them to be separate and lay them on a chair. Then you tie the other three together in a string.

'These handkerchiefs are all brothers and sisters,' you say. 'They all came out of the same box. So whatever I do to these three, the other three will copy it.'

You pick up the handkerchiefs from the chair and sure enough they are tied in a string like the others.

HOW TO DO IT

Take three handkerchiefs and tie them in a string. Now pick up each handkerchief by a corner next to the tied corner. They will then hang down and hide the knots. Figure 1. To make sure, hold the three handkerchiefs in your left hand, round their middles. The other three handkerchiefs, which must be the same size and colour as the first three, you also hold in your left hand.

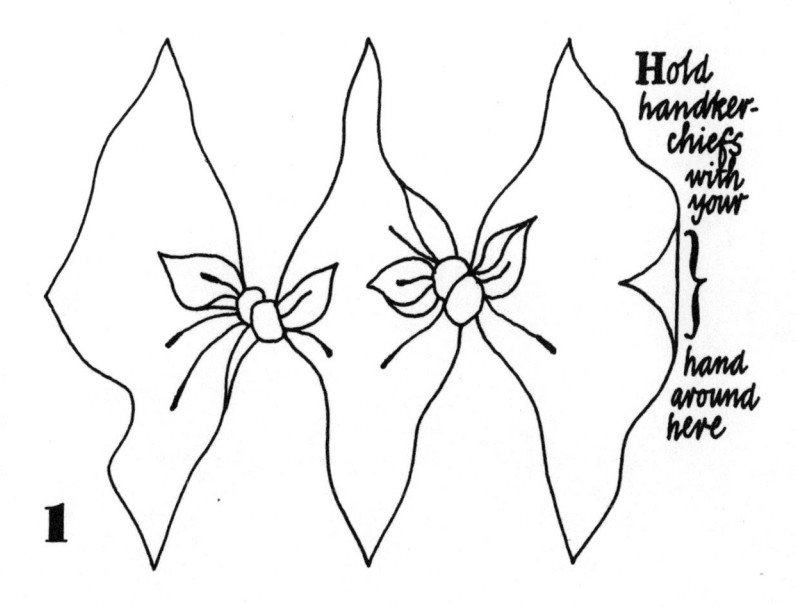

Take the three loose handkerchiefs one at a time in your right hand. Say, 'I'm going to put these three handkerchiefs on this chair.' Turn to your right, bring your hands together and put on the chair the three tied handkerchiefs in your left hand. As the audience don't know what you're going to do they'll be quite satisfied that you've put three loose handkerchiefs on the chair.

Now show the same three loose handkerchiefs that you started with and tie them in a string. Then all you have to do is pick up the handkerchiefs from the chair and they will be seen to be tied together.

Please remember that in this trick all the handkerchiefs must look alike, or otherwise the awful audience will notice that you haven't put on the chair the same handkerchiefs that you showed separate.

More Advanced Magic

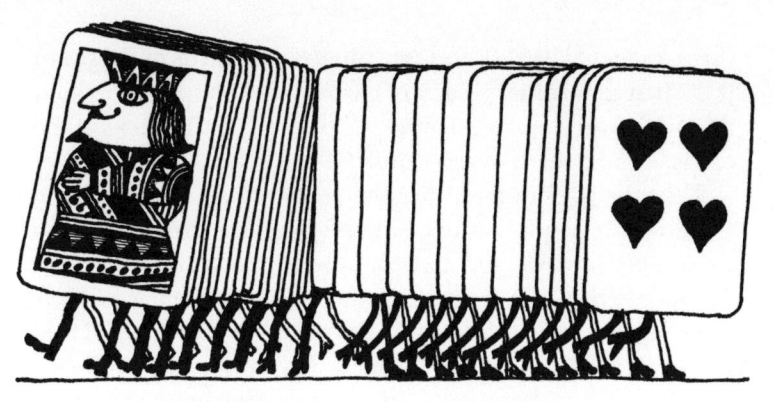

Follow my Leader

This is a card trick, but a rather unusual one. The effect, for a card trick, is quite big.

You count out from the pack twelve plain spot cards and put them in a heap, face down, with the top card face up. At the other side of the table you count out the twelve picture cards, or court cards as they are called, also face down with the top one face up.

'This is a game of "follow my leader",' you say. You take the top court card from the heap of court cards and put it on top of the plain cards. And you transfer the top plain card to the heap of court cards.

'Did you see them follow?' you ask. 'I don't suppose you did because they did it rather invisibly. But they did it all the same.' You spread out the packet that was plain cards and the audience see that they are now all court cards, while the packet that was court cards are now all plain.

HOW TO DO IT

You need a pack of cards. Not a special conjurer's pack with eighty-two cards, nine aces of spades, five queens of hearts, three and a half jokers and two picture postcards of Brighton pier. Just an ordinary pack of cards, but it must be the kind that has a white margin round the pattern on the backs of the cards. You'll see why presently.

Take the pack and remove the twelve court cards, putting them in a neat pile on one side of the table. Next count off twelve plain cards and put them in a pile beside the court cards. Then, while reminding the audience what you have done, secretly turn the bottom card of the pack over. Hold the pack in your left hand, low down so that the audience cannot catch a glimpse of the reversed bottom card.

You now explain that you will put the two packets of cards together so that they can get to know each other better. Pick up the twelve court cards, display them in a fan or hand them to someone to verify that there are just twelve court cards. Place this packet on top of the pack.

Now pick up the packet of plain cards. As you do this drop your left hand to your side and secretly turn the pack over. This isn't difficult, but practise it a few times so that you can do it smoothly and secretly. Then put the packet of plain cards on what is really the bottom of the pack. The single reversed card will disguise the fact that the pack has been turned over.

Now you see why the cards must be the kind that have a white margin round the pattern on the backs. If the coloured back went all over the cards the fact that a card or cards are facing the opposite way to the others would be noticeable, because a bit of the white faces of the reversed cards would show against the coloured backs. As long as there is a white margin round the backs of the cards and you handle the pack carefully, nobody can tell that some cards have been reversed.

Explain to the audience that you have put the twelve court

cards on the pack and put the twelve plain cards on top of them. You haven't, of course, but that's the sort of untruth conjurers are allowed to tell. You explain that the two packets of cards, being together, now arrive at an understanding. You don't say what the understanding is because you don't know.

Take the top card of the pack. It is, of course, one of the plain cards you have just put there. Lay it face upwards on one side of the table. As you do this, lower your left hand and turn the pack over secretly again, bringing the court cards to the top. Proceed to count off eleven more cards, face down. Put them beside the plain card on the table.

'On this side of the table we have twelve plain cards,' you say. 'And I have left one face up to remind you that these are the plain cards.' (Actually of course they are eleven court cards with one plain card face up.)

Now take the next card. It is, of course, the twelfth court card but the audience will think it is the first of the packet of court cards. Put it on the other side of the table, face up. As you count eleven more cards beside it, the audience think that these are the remaining eleven court cards, but they are really plain cards.

Put the rest of the pack aside into a box or somewhere out of reach of the audience, so that they cannot discover that some of the cards are reversed.

You now explain that the cards, having arrived at an understanding, will follow one another. You take the face up court card and the face up plain card and put them on the opposite packets. You can then show that the rest of the cards have apparently followed their leader and all the court cards are where the plain cards were, and vice versa, which is Branestawm language for the other way round.

These directions may sound complicated but if you follow

them with a pack of cards in your hand you'll find it quite easy. Let's recap, as they say somewhere or other, and do the whole thing by numbers:

1. Count out twelve court cards on to the table, face up.
2. Count out twelve plain cards beside them, face up.
3. Secretly reverse the bottom card of the pack.
4. Put the twelve court cards on top of the pack.
5. Turn the pack over secretly.
6. Put the twelve plain cards on what is really the bottom of the pack.
7. Take the top card (a plain one) and lay it on the table.
8. Secretly turn the pack over.
9. Count out eleven more cards. (They're court cards but the audience think they are the plain ones they've just seen you put there.) Lay them face down beside the plain card on the table.
10. Take the next card (it will be a court card) and put it face up on the other side of the table.
11. Count out eleven more cards face down beside it. (The audience will think they are the rest of the court cards but they are really plain ones.)
12. Put the pack aside.

Now all you have to do is change over the two face up cards and show that the rest of the cards have apparently followed their leader.

Quite an astonishing effect. And it's easy, but you must practise it a bit so as to remember what to do at each stage.

As a matter of fact it's actually easier to do this trick than to describe how to do it. That means it's easier to be a magician than to be an author. Isn't life rum?

The Ghost Writer

There is actually a bit of conjuring about the title of this trick. A ghost writer is really a professional writer who writes a book for someone else, under that person's name. Famous people sometimes employ ghost writers to write the story of their lives if they can't spell much or are absolutely useless at grammar. But this trick is about a different kind of ghost writer.

You begin the trick by showing a blank card which you seal in an envelope. The envelope is then sealed in a larger one and this in turn is sealed in a third envelope. All the envelopes are marked by a member of the audience.

Next you take a book and ask someone to push a playing card in to mark a page. The book is opened at the marked page and a word is chosen, from either page, according to the number of spots on the card. For instance, if it is a seven, the seventh word on the page is taken, ignoring the title at the top of the page.

The three sealed envelopes are then opened and the marks made by a member of the audience are still on them. In the smallest envelope the card is found and on it is written, in suitably ghostly writing, the very word chosen from the book.

HOW TO DO IT

You present this trick by saying that you have a ghost in your pocket. You take out a piece of nothing and say, 'Here is my pocket ghost. He's very handsome, isn't he? Absolutely out of this world, in fact. We'll stand him on the table for a moment while I show you what he is going to do, so keep an eye on him.'

You pretend to put the invisible something on the table. You pick up a plain card, show it both sides and put it into an envelope which you slide into a slightly bigger envelope. Now inside this bigger envelope is a similar card with the word that is going to be chosen written on it. Ah, how do you know what word is going to be chosen? I'll tell you that in a minute, but we'll suppose the word is 'thought'. The card with this word written on it is in a duplicate envelope inside the larger one. When you slide in the envelope with the blank card in it, you slide it right behind the other small envelope, and draw the other envelope partly out. Figure 1.

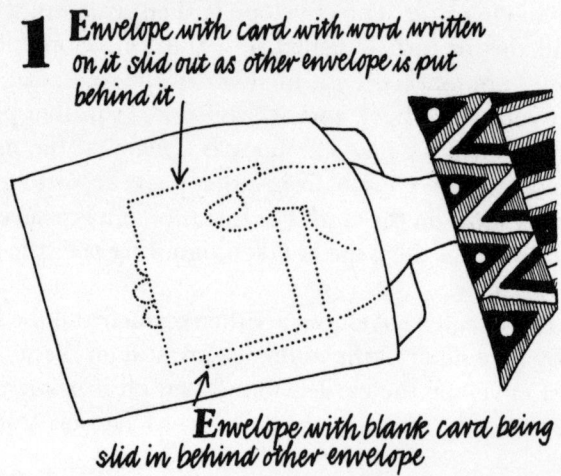

1 *Envelope with card with word written on it slid out as other envelope is put behind it*

Envelope with blank card being slid in behind other envelope

'I nearly forgot to put my pocket ghost in with the card,' you say. You lift the flap of the envelope and pretend to put the invisible nothing into it. Then you seal the envelope and ask a member of the audience to mark it. They will, of course, be marking the envelope that contains the card with the word written on it, but they don't know that.

Now seal the outer envelope and have it marked. Then put that into a slightly larger envelope, seal it and have that marked too. Leave the nest of envelopes with the member of the audience who has marked them.

After the word has been chosen you say, 'I shall now ask my pocket ghost writer to write the name of the chosen word on the card in the envelope with him.' Pause a moment, then say, 'Have you written it, ghost? Yes, the pocket ghost says he has written it and hopes he's spelt it right.'

You ask the person holding the nest of envelopes to make sure his mark is on the outer envelope. Then you ask him to open the envelope and give you the one inside. You show that this envelope also bears his mark, slit it open and take out the smallest envelope. But of course you take out the one containing the card with the word written on it. You know which of the two envelopes this is because it will be the one farthest away from the address side. Take it out and give it to the person helping you and ask him to make sure it still has his mark on it. Casually crumple the envelope with the duplicate in it and toss it into a box out of the way. You then ask the person who marked the envelopes to open the smallest envelope and read out what the ghost writer has written. This turns out to be the chosen word.

Right, now how to make sure one particular word is chosen, so that you can write it on the card when you prepare for the trick before the show?

First you want a book which has one page entirely occupied by an illustration and this page must be either near the end or near the beginning of the book. You will find such a page on page 129 of the hard cover edition of *Professor Branestawm's Treasure Hunt*. You will also find it on page 177 of the paperback edition. But you shouldn't have much difficulty in finding a suitable page in some other book if you don't have either of those.

Let's assume you choose page 129 of the hard cover edition

of *Professor Branestawm's Treasure Hunt*. The word 'thought' is the ninth word on the top line of this page. The opposite page is entirely occupied with a drawing of Maisie and Daisie in their cars, so we don't have to worry about them – let their dad, the Vicar, do the worrying.

You take a card with nine pips, it doesn't matter which suit, and place it in the book at page 129.

You are now ready to have the word chosen. Bring the book forward and hand a playing card to someone in the audience. It will, of course, be a duplicate of the nine spot card you have already put in the book. If you want to have the card chosen I'll tell you in a minute or two how to do that and still make sure the nine is chosen.

Ask the member of the audience to push the card into the book. Hold the book so that the card is pushed in somewhere above where your duplicate card is. Figure 2. You then open the book at the page where you put the card, namely page 129 in this case. Say, 'How many spots are there on the card? Nine. Then will you please count to the ninth word on either page, ignoring the title at the top.'

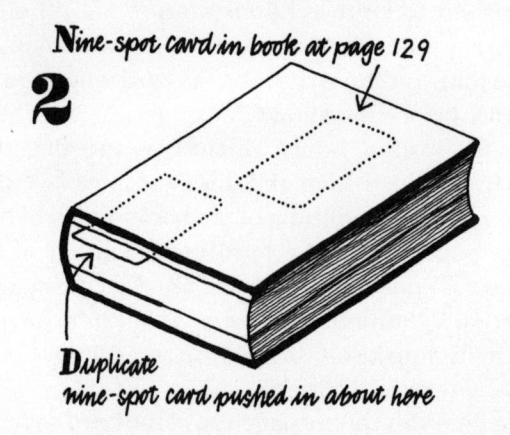

Nine-spot card in book at page 129

2

Duplicate nine-spot card pushed in about here

Hold the book open and hold it firmly so that the other card doesn't drop out. The member of the audience will have to count to the ninth word on page 129 because there aren't any words on the other page. But the audience don't know there are words only on one page and most of them will think the person choosing the word has a free choice of either page. He counts to the ninth word and reads out the word 'thought'.

Having made sure that the audience know what the chosen word is, you then proceed to open the envelopes as I have already described, and reveal the chosen word written on the card by your ghost writer.

Don't forget to put the invisible ghost writer back in your pocket afterwards or the audience may think you a bit unkind leaving him out in the cold.

I promised to tell you how to make sure the number you want to use can be chosen from the pack when the choice seems to be free.

← Press top card of pack to slip it into lower half of pack.

3

Have the card you want chosen, on top of the pack. Riffle the cards and ask someone to put a finger in somewhere in the pack as the cards are riffled past. Open the pack bookwise at this point, draw it away from the person's hand and lift off the top half of the pack. But in doing this you press with the fingers of your left hand on to the top card. This will cause the top card to slide on to the bottom half of the pack as you take the top half away. You then offer the top card of the bottom half, which will, of course, seem to be the card where the member of the audience put his finger in the pack. Figure 3.

The Great Crown Jewel Swop

One of the nice things about magic is that very often you can do several quite different tricks, using exactly the same method. This one is a good example. The method is the same as that used for producing a name on a card, sealed in three marked envelopes, in 'The Ghost Writer' but the effect is quite different.

You explain that the Queen of Incrediblania was a bit tired of the crown jewels. 'They're so usual,' she said. 'And not exciting any more. They're like part of the wallpaper. I know them as well as I know my own nose.' She knew her nose very well because she used to powder it a lot. The King said he couldn't help that, the kingdom couldn't afford new crown jewels just because the Queen powdered her nose a lot. But it so happened that the Queen of Crashbania was just as fed up with her crown jewels. So the two Queens decided to swop crown jewels and this is how they did it.

You show a piece of card cut out in the shape of a crown, painted gold or covered with gold foil, with bits of red foil on it for rubies. Figure 1. 'These are the crown jewels of Incrediblania,' you explain. Then you show another flat cardboard crown of a different shape, covered with silver foil and pieces of green foil for emeralds. Figure 2.

1 — *Cardboard painted gold* — *Red foil*

The Crown of Incrediblania (make 2 alike)

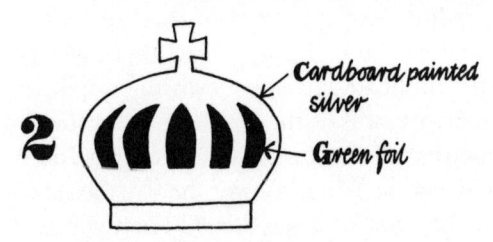

2 — *Cardboard painted silver* — *Green foil*

The Crown of Crashbania (make 2 alike)

You then ask a lady in the audience to be the Queen of Incrediblania and to help you. You put the Incrediblanian crown into an envelope, seal it, put it in another envelope and that into a third envelope. The lady initials each envelope with a red pencil.

You now get another lady to be the Queen of Crashbania and you put the Crashbanian crown into another set of envelopes which the lady marks with a green pencil.

'The great Crown Jewel Swop will now take place,' you say. You can blow a sort of a fanfare on a toy trumpet, if you like, or wave some flags or do any other funny business that occurs to you to mark this incredible royal occasion.

When the envelopes are opened the Incrediblanian crown with the red jewels is found in the nest of envelopes marked green and the Crashbanian jewels are found in the envelopes marked red.

HOW TO DO IT

Well, you know, don't you, unless you haven't read 'The Ghost Writer'.

You need two Incrediblanian crowns exactly alike and two Crashbanian crowns. One Incrediblanian crown is in an envelope, sealed, inside the second size envelope. And one Crashbanian crown is also already in envelopes in the same way. Keep the two sets of envelopes on tables at opposite sides of the stage or room.

The Incrediblanian crown goes into an empty envelope, which is then slid into the next size envelope. This already contains the duplicate envelope with the duplicate Crashbanian crown in it. You slide the envelope under the Crashbanian one. You then ask the lady who is the Queen of Incrediblania to mark the envelopes. You draw out the Crashbanian one and it is this envelope that is marked red. Then you seal the outer envelope and have it marked red, and enclose it in the third envelope which is also marked red.

You do exactly the same with the other set of envelopes so that it is really the duplicate Incrediblanian crown that is in the green marked envelope.

Do the trumpet fanfare or flag-waving business, ask the lady being Queen of Incrediblania to open the red marked envelope and give you the one inside. Show the red marks on this, open it and take out the red marked envelope. Give this to the Queen lady to open and shove the envelope out of the way.

Now do exactly the same with the other nest of envelopes and there you are.

Sensational Vanishing Alarm Clock

This is a lovely trick to start a show. Done well it will get you a huge round of applause.

All it amounts to is this. You pick up a ringing alarm clock and throw it into the air, when it instantly changes to a shower of confetti. Clock, noise and all, has vanished into the thinnest air they have in stock.

HOW TO DO IT

Ha! you may say, or even, Ho! A collapsible alarm clock that whangs up your sleeve and knocks your eyebrows crooked? Or mechanical trapdoors and invisible elastic wires? No, no. I'm sorry to disappoint you but all you need for this trick is an ordinary alarm clock, a handful of confetti and a special kind of bag which you can make quite easily.

The clock stands on a small table, which should be higher than the usual kind of table. If you can't find a tall table, use an ordinary small table and put an empty box on it. The box should be laid on its side with the open part facing the audience so that they can see it doesn't contain any traps or mechanism.

The clock stands on the table or on the box. Just in front of the table and a little to the left is a chair. To the back of this chair is fastened the special bag I mentioned. To make the bag, take a wire coat hanger, bend it out to form a sort of rectangle and then bend the hook part up almost at right angles, as shown in Figure 1. Now make a bag of dark material, preferably black because by conjurer's rules anything black is invisible. Sew the bag to the wire frame as in Figure 2. The bag must be deep enough to take the clock easily.

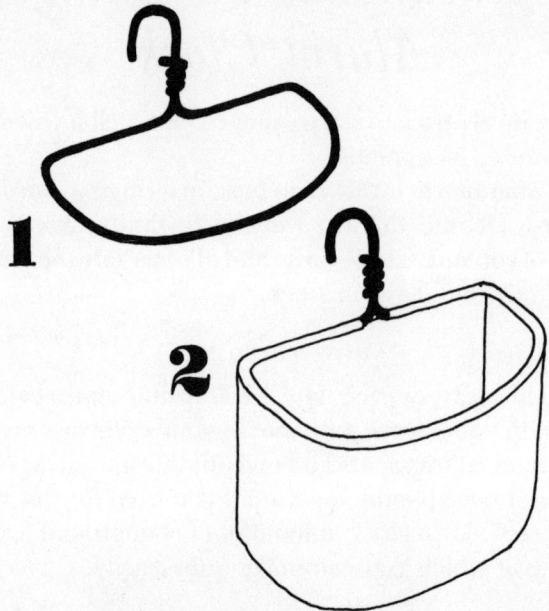

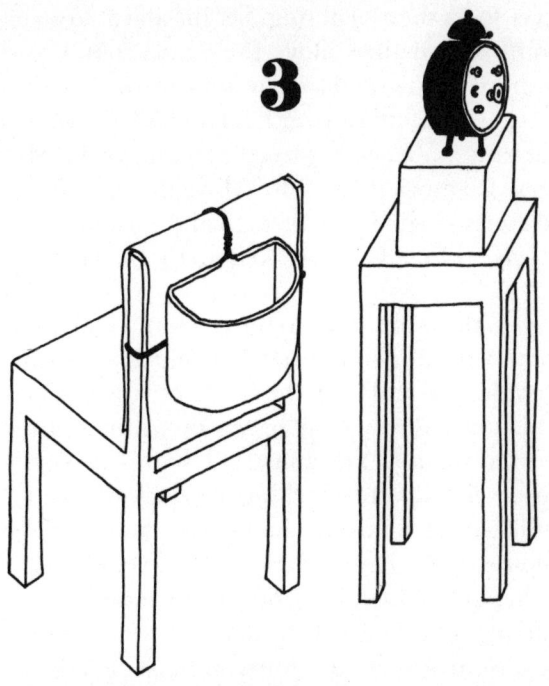

Hang this bag on the back of the chair, adjusting the angle of the hook so that the bag is level and horizontal. A chair with a solid back is best but if your chair has an open back, throw a cloth or scarf over the back to hide the bag. Put the cloth over the chair back first, then hook the bag over it. The bit of wire hook showing won't be noticed but, if you're afraid it will be, just lay a handkerchief over it.

If your chair has an open back and the bag tends to swing in under it, you must take another piece of stiff wire, or a piece of wood, and tie it firmly along the back of the bag. This will keep the bag in position. Figure 3 shows this and also how the table and chair are arranged.

Now you are all ready. Wind up the alarm and move the

little lever to let the alarm ring. Set the alarm to go off at any time you like and then move the hands round so that the alarm isn't due to go off for an hour or so.

Have some confetti in your left hand. Come on, with your left side to the audience. Go to the clock and say, 'My clock is a bit slow. I'll move it on a bit.' Move the hands round until the bell starts ringing. Move back and turn to the audience and say, 'Next time you're woken up by an alarm clock, just do this.'

You go to the table, pick up the clock and make a throwing movement with it. As your hands come down for the throw switch off the bell and drop the clock into the bag behind the chair. Instantly throw your hands up again and throw the confetti into the air. You must follow this movement with your eyes as if you were watching the clock go up into the air. The audience will follow the movement, and the appearance of the confetti, the disappearance of the clock and the fact that the bell stops ringing, all produce a perfect illusion of the clock having vanished in mid air.

This is quite easy to do, but you must practise it well so that you can do the throwing movement neatly and naturally. You can give a quick glance down as you throw the clock into the bag but you must immediately make the upward throwing movement and follow it with your eyes. Remember, too, to practise picking up the clock with one finger over the lever that stops the bell. But, even if you fail to stop the bell, the bag will muffle it so much that nobody in the audience will be able to hear it, particularly as the applause will drown it anyway.

This trick is perfect for performing in a hall and you can even do it in a large room.

After the applause dies down you can say, 'That's one way of passing the time.'

The Dieter

You show a large dice, about 8 cm square, black with white spots. It rests on a plate. You also show a little doll and explain that the doll is on a diet. In fact it is a dieter or, in other words, a die eater, and, since the correct name for one dice is a die, that's why the die is on a plate.

You put the doll on top of the die and cover them both with a tube of cardboard.

'We'll give the dieter a moment or two to eat the die,' you say. Then you lift the cover and there is the doll on the plate and the die has completely vanished.

HOW TO DO IT

You want two small dolls both alike. The die is hollow and one side is missing. To make it, mark out a piece of stiff card as shown in Figure 1. Cut away the four parts marked A and score part way through the card along the four lines marked B.

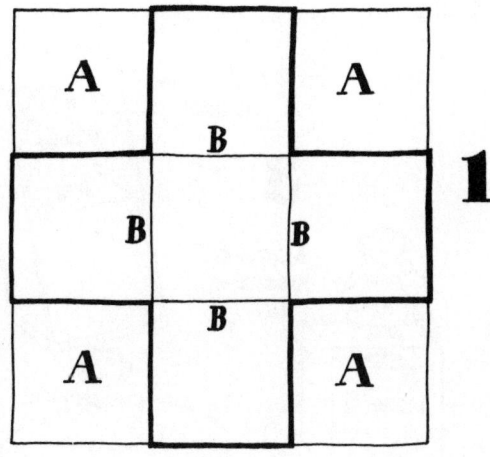

2

Fold up the four side squares to make a square box and tape the sides together. Paint the whole thing black and stick white spots on it. You can buy small white gummed spots at most stationers. To make a proper die the spots on opposite sides must add up to seven. If you imagine the missing side is a one spot, then the top of the die, when it is placed open side down, will be the six spot. This arrangement of spots doesn't affect the trick but you might as well make the die properly.

To prepare for the trick put one of the dolls on a plate and put the hollow die over it.

3

First doll hidden in tube

Second doll hidden in die

Bring on the plate with the die and explain that it's on a plate because the doll – here you show the other doll – is on a diet or, in other words, is a die eater.

Put the doll on top of the die and say that the doll will now eat the die, but you are going to cover it so that the doll can have its dinner in private.

You cover die and doll with a cardboard tube. This tube is made by scoring a piece of cardboard and folding it into a square tube just large enough to slide easily over the die. Tape the sides together and, if you like, cover the tube with fancy paper. The tube should be high enough so that, when it is placed over the die and doll, both are concealed.

To make the die vanish, lift the tube near the bottom, squeezing the sides so as to pick up the hollow die inside the cover. Lift it off, when of course the doll on top of the die will come with it and the duplicate doll will be revealed sitting on the plate. The die has vanished. See Figure 3.

'You will notice,' you say, 'that the doll isn't any fatter after eating that big die. That's because, as I said, it's on a diet.'

The Wonderful Stick

You won't believe this. A black stick about 60 cm long that will cause a handkerchief to appear, make a handkerchief disappear, or make it change colour, *zip*, just like that!

Here is the astonishing secret.

The stick isn't a stick, but a length of tubing. It can be a piece of plastic tubing, which is the best kind if you can get it. There are shops that sell plastic tubing and you want a piece about 2 cm in diameter. If you can't get plastic tubing, a length of chromium-plated curtain rod, which is really tube, will do, and you may be able to get a short piece like this quite cheaply. But whatever kind of tube you use, the inside must be quite smooth.

Having got your tube the first thing to do is to make a wooden plug to fit tightly into one end. To make sure the plug can't come out it is as well to make a small hole about 4 or 5 cm from the end of the tube and put a screw through this hole into the plug. But before you screw the plug in, put a small screw eye into the end of the plug that goes inside the tube. Then tie one end of a long piece of strong elastic to the screw eye. Now thread the elastic through the tube, push the plug into the tube and fix it in place with the screw. Leave a little of the screw projecting. See Figure 1.

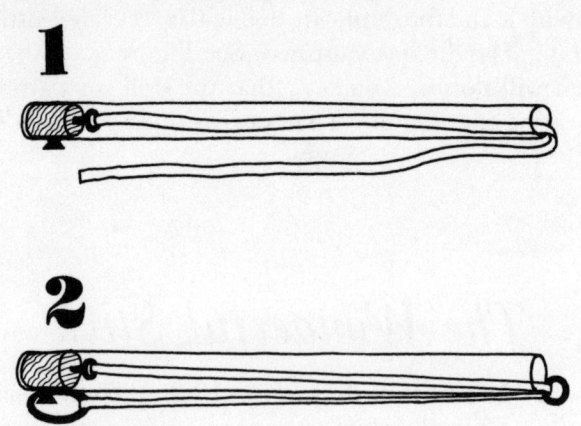

1

2

Now take the elastic and pull it out of the tube as far as it will go, stretching it quite tight. At the point where it comes out of the tube tie a small metal ring. This ring must be small enough to go easily into the tube.

Now stretch the elastic again so that when the small ring is at the lip of the tube, the rest of the elastic is stretched down to the other end of the tube, on the outside. Tie a ring to the elastic where it reaches the plugged end of the tube, when fully stretched. This ring must be large enough so that it won't go into the tube. Cut off the rest of the elastic and your wonderful stick is ready. See Figure 2.

To set the stick, stretch the elastic until the small ring comes on the edge of the tube, then stretch it down and slip the large ring over the projecting screw at the plugged end of the tube, as shown in Figure 2.

TO MAKE A HANDKERCHIEF VANISH Simply tuck the handkerchief (a small silk one, of course) through the small ring. Hold the stick by the plugged end with the handkerchief on the other end of it. Keep the side of the stick with the elastic held away from the audience. To make the handkerchief vanish, push the large ring off the projecting screw and, *zim*! the elastic will whip the handkerchief into the tube like lightning. The large ring, being too big to go into the tube, will stop close up to the open end of the tube and the audience will, of course, think they are still seeing the small ring. You can re-set the stick and get the vanished handkerchief out again by pulling on the large ring.

TO MAKE A HANDKERCHIEF APPEAR Pull the elastic right out, as before. Tuck the handkerchief through the large ring, bunch it up and hold it in the hand that holds the stick but don't slip the ring over the projecting screw this time. Wave the stick about, let go of the handkerchief, and it will fly to the end of the stick and appear apparently from nowhere.

TO MAKE A HANDKERCHIEF CHANGE COLOUR Set the stick as for the appearing handkerchief. Come on holding the stick, take a silk handkerchief of a different colour from the concealed one, and put it through the small ring. Wave the stick, release the hidden handkerchief and *wowzie*! or other excitable noises, the visible handkerchief will disappear inside the tube and the different-coloured one will fly up to take its place.

One word of warning. Don't hold the stick near anyone's face when you use it because the elastic will swing the large ring outwards as it flies to the end of the stick and could hit someone a nasty smack.

P.S. (Meaning perhapsible suggestion) If you can't get any silk fine enough to make handkerchiefs that will go easily into the hollow stick, you can use pieces of ribbon a few centimetres wide.

Double Colour-Changing Handkerchiefs

In *Norman Hunter's Book of Magic*, I described a special kind of silk handkerchief which changed colour when you passed your hand down it. Here is another kind of colour-changing handkerchief, only this time there are two handkerchiefs tied together, and they both change colour when you pass a hand down them. And what's more, both handkerchiefs can be of different colours and both can change colour.

Very easy to make. First you want two squares of silk or, if you can't get silk, some thin, soft, silky material. These should be about 30 cm square and you fasten them together by one corner. Don't tie them because the knot makes an inconvenient lump; simply sew them together. We will suppose one is red and one is yellow. See Figure 1.

Next you take two more squares of different colours from

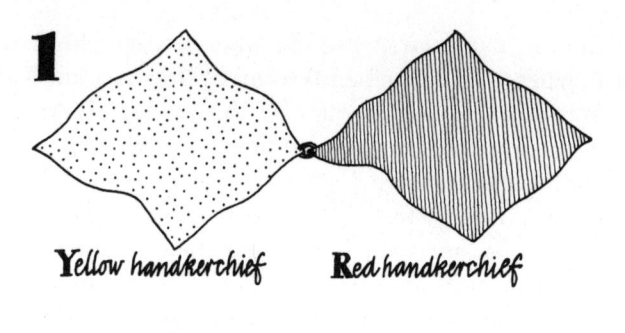

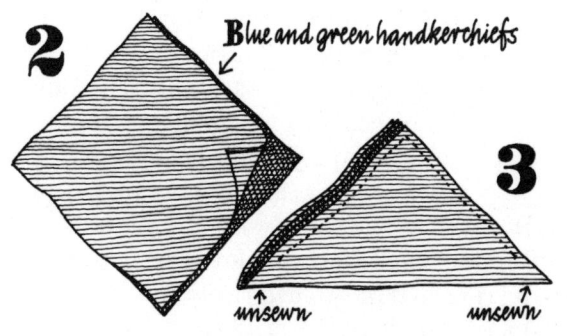

1

Yellow handkerchief *Red handkerchief*

2

Blue and green handkerchiefs

3

unsewn *unsewn*

those of the other handkerchiefs. Shall we say one blue and one green. Lay one on top of the other, fold them diagonally and sew along the two edges, but leave a gap of a few centimetres at each corner. See Figures 2 and 3.

Now you take this sort of triangular bag handkerchief and slide it over the other two handkerchiefs until it entirely covers one handkerchief, say the yellow one, as in Figure 4.

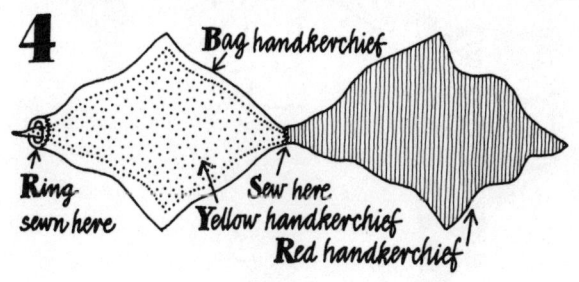

4

Bag handkerchief

Ring sewn here *Sew here.*
Yellow handkerchief
Red handkerchief

Sew the bag handkerchief to the other handkerchiefs at the corner where the other handkerchiefs already join. Take a metal curtain ring large enough for the handkerchiefs to pass through easily and sew this into the open opposite corner of the bag handkerchief.

You now have what looks like two handkerchiefs tied together, a blue one (which is the bag handkerchief with the blue side showing) and a red one. Hold the ring of the bag handkerchief in one hand and with the other hold the corner of the yellow handkerchief that is inside it. Pull the ring right down. The bag handkerchief will turn inside out, showing its green side. And it will cover the red handkerchief and expose the yellow one. So instead of a blue and a red handkerchief, you now have a green and a yellow one. Figure 5. Isn't that nice?

One little point. When you sew the ring in the corner of the bag handkerchief, tuck a fair amount of the bag handkerchief through the ring so that you can easily get hold of the single handkerchief inside it.

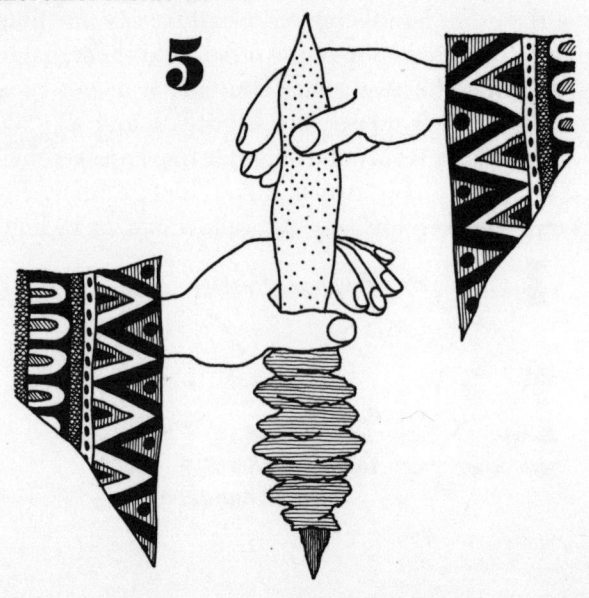

Colourology

This is a sort of Professor Branestawm lecture with magical illustrations. What you need for it are three sets of double colour-changing handkerchiefs, as described in the last item.

One double colour-change handkerchief should change from yellow and blue handkerchiefs to two green ones. Another should change from red and blue handkerchiefs to two purple ones and the third should change from red and yellow handkerchiefs to two orange ones.

At the start have the double colour-change handkerchiefs showing yellow and blue on one, red and blue on another and red and yellow on the third.

'This,' you say, 'is a lecture on colourology which Professor Branestawm was to have given at Pagwell University but he lost the way and arrived at Lower Pagwell Jam and Marmalade Works by mistake. The purpose of the lecture is to show how the primary colours combine to make secondary colours. This sounds pretty boring when you say it but it's quite fun when you do it.'

You pick up the yellow and blue handkerchiefs.

'Here are two handkerchiefs, one yellow and one blue. If these two primary colours are combined they make green.'

You stroke your hand down the handkerchiefs and turn them into green ones.

'In the same way,' you go on, picking up the red and blue handkerchiefs, 'if you combine red and blue you get purple.'

Stroke the red and blue handkerchiefs and change them to two purple ones.

'Finally,' you say, 'a combination of red and yellow will give you orange.' You stroke the red and yellow handkerchiefs and change them to two orange ones.

'People who don't like oranges should abandon this experiment and do the disappearing banana, which is easier because you just eat it.'

You can then carry your colourology lecture to its logical conclusion by putting all the purple, orange and green handkerchiefs into a box and turning them into one large white one.

'If you mix all the colours together,' you explain, 'they cancel each other out and you get white, or more probably a murky grey.'

To do this you need a box without a lid. You can make this quite easily from cardboard. It should be about 21 cm high and 14 cm wide. Cut out a piece of stiff cardboard as shown in Figure 1. Score the divisions part way through on one side so that you can bend the sides and bottom into a tall square box. But before you do this, cut another piece of cardboard the teeniest bit less than 14 cm wide and 21 cm long. Fasten this with sticky tape across the centre of the bottom of the box so that when the box is made up this piece will come inside. Figure 2. Now fold up the sides and bottom of the box and tape the joins. After that you can either paint the box or cover it with fancy paper. It is also a good idea to paint the inside of the box and both sides of the flap black. Do this before you make up the box.

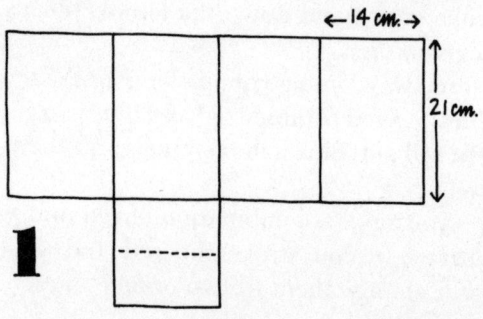

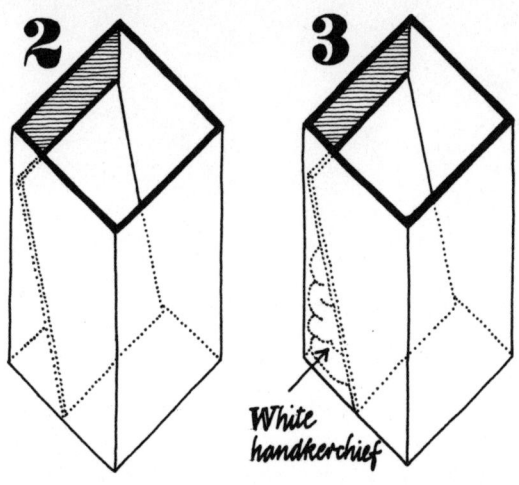

Now, to change the coloured handkerchiefs to a white one, have a large white, or if you like, murky grey, handkerchief in the box on one side of the flap and fold the flap over to cover it. Figure 3. Show the box empty by holding the flap against the side with your fingers. Just give the audience a quick glance into it, then push the coloured handkerchiefs in and swing the flap over to cover them and release the white one. Figure 4. Say your piece, take out the white or murky grey handkerchief, and again show the box empty.

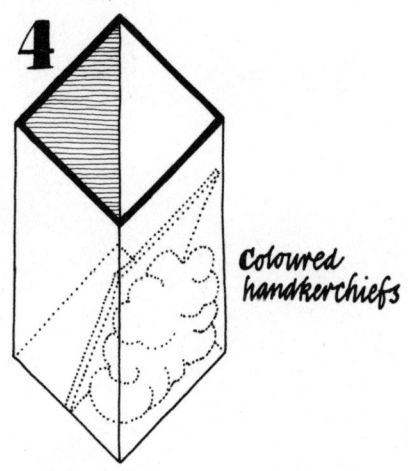

Magic with People

Magic with People

Doing magic with people is very much the same as doing magic with things, but not quite the same. You can make a lady vanish from a box by using a bigger box than you would use for vanishing a ball or a handkerchief. But you can't pull a lady up your sleeve on a bit of elastic as you can a silk handkerchief, neither can you palm a lady or pretend to put her in one hand while really keeping her in the other. And ladies don't take kindly to being crumpled up in double papers or folded up and concealed in a fold of your coat sleeve, all of which you can do with the other things used in conjuring.

But ha! There is one big advantage in conjuring with people. People can move about and put themselves into secret hiding places instead of the conjurer having to do it as he does with inanimate objects. This means that you can show a screen, for instance, on both sides, and then produce a girl from it, because the girl can move about behind the screen in such a way that the audience never see her until you are ready to produce her.

Doing magic with people, of course, means that you need people. You can't do it by yourself. If you are going to vanish a lady you need a lady to vanish. And you will also need two or possibly more assistants to help you move the apparatus about in presenting the magic.

So this section on 'Magic with People' really ties up with what I said in my first *Book of Magic* about 'Group Magic', meaning doing a magic show with the help of friends or classmates. You can put on a very interesting show for a school concert, for instance, by doing some tricks with handkerchiefs, cards and so on and interspersing these with a piece of bigger magic, using a girl or boy.

This is the best way to arrange such a show. On your stage, or on that part of the floor you are going to use as a stage, you want a curtain that can be drawn to hide the back part of the stage. This curtain should be about two metres from the front of the stage, so that you can perform tricks there while others are being prepared behind the curtain. The curtain need not necessarily divide in the centre as curtains on big stages do. It can simply draw across to one side.

To save you getting in a fearful tangle with cords and pulleys and things, here is the correct and simple way to arrange the cording of a divided curtain. You use only one cord. It goes over a pulley at one side of the stage, across to the other side of the stage, round another pulley there, then back to the first side and over another pulley. You want to tie small weights to the two ends of the cord to keep it from sagging and to prevent one end from getting drawn up through the pulley and coming loose.

Your two curtains are hung in the usual way with hooks on a curtain rail or with rings on a rod. You fasten the outer ends of the curtains at the top of the rod or rail. Then, with the curtains closed, you attach the top inner corner of one curtain to one part of the cord and the top inner corner of the other curtain to the other part of the cord. See opposite.

To be really satisfactory the two curtains should overlap a little in the centre when drawn together. You can do this by using the special fittings sold for cord sets by shops that sell curtain equipment. Or you can have two rods fixed parallel to each other and hang one curtain on one rod and one on the other.

If you decide to do it the simpler way and just have one

curtain to draw right across to one side, the cording arrangement is exactly the same and you fix one end of the curtain to the rail at the outer side and fix the other top corner of the curtain to either part of the cord.

Now, this is the way to use the curtain in running the show.

To begin with, the curtain is closed and your stage is set with a quick people-magic item, such as 'The Girl from Nowhere', with your assistants standing in their places as described for that item. Play some nice, loud, short, trumpety music on a record or tape, open the curtain, and come on and make your bow. Show the box, produce the girl and as the audience applaud, walk forward and have the curtain closed behind you. At the same time an assistant walks on with a small table on which are the things for one or two tricks. You perform these tricks and, while you are doing them, your other assistants set up another piece of people-magic behind the curtain. When you have done the small tricks, your assistants carry the table off, the curtain opens and you do the people-magic item. Then the curtain closes and you do more small tricks in front of it. Work the show like this and finish with a suitable piece of magic with people, such as 'Professor Flittersnoop and Mrs Branestawm,' described at the end of this book.

Arranged in this way, your magic show will run smoothly. Your assistants will have plenty of time to prepare behind the curtain, and the whole entertainment will have a really professional look.

Now about your assistants. They should all look as alike as possible, so choose boys or girls about the same height and colouring. They could wear blue jeans and red jerseys, for instance. Scout or guide uniform is fine, of course, but any kind of simple dress will do as long as all the assistants look pretty much alike. There are two reasons for this. In the first place the assistants all looking alike and the performer being dressed differently will give him or her more importance. And in the second place, in some magical effects it is useful if the audience don't know which particular assistant they are looking at, as you will see in 'The Haunted Tower' explained in this section.

Then about the girl to be produced and vanished. Magicians usually have a girl for this because it looks more attractive to produce a pretty girl from a box than to haul out a boy with scraggy hair and big ears, or even a boy with neat hair and small ears. And girls usually tend to fold up smaller than boys. But of course you don't have to follow tradition in this way. You can produce a boy or vanish a boy or use a boy for any of these pieces of people-magic. In fact, you might like to use a boy for some of them and a girl for others.

The girl or boy you use as a box jumper – the professional name for the person who appears and disappears in magical items – should be small, slim and agile. The smaller he or she is, the more easily he or she can pack into the secret part of a box and the smaller the box can be. But your boy or girl must be able to leap out of the box nice and quickly, so don't pick a very little girl or boy who is only just old enough to walk.

Now you will probably be waving your hands about and saying, 'What about the boxes?' Of course, I'm not going to suggest that you go carpentering up enormous boxes out of wood for these pieces of magic. It would be too expensive, too difficult and too cumbersome. But fortunately there are nice large, light-weight boxes all ready waiting for you to pick up. You know the big, cardboard cartons that packets of breakfast cereal and so on arrive in at the supermarkets? Well, they are just what you want and if you speak nicely to the manager of your local supermarket or grocer's and tell him what you want the boxes for, I think you'll find he'll be quite pleased to get rid of some. You might also try your local furniture shop and shops that sell refrigerators and cookers, because these items also come in big cardboard cartons, which the shop often throws away.

I have explained in the following pages how to prepare boxes of this kind for the magic. You can paint the boxes in bright colours or cover them with fancy paper, or, of course, you can use them just as they are. They don't look so attractive like that, but on the other hand they do look as if they are just ordinary boxes and not specially prepared for magic, which helps to make the magic more effective.

And now for the dire secrets of how to abolish pretty young ladies or produce them out of fairly thin air, at will.

The Girl from Nowhere

On your stage or platform, or floor of the Scout Hall, or wherever, you have two large cardboard cartons, one inside the other. They are lying on their sides with the openings facing the audience. The lids are open and the audience can see the inner box is empty, and, as you close its lid and slide it into the larger box, it is clear that that box must be empty too or the other box wouldn't go into it.

You stand the boxes upright, clap your hands, fire a cap pistol, ring a bell, blow a whistle or utter a frightful spell and *voilà*! or other continental noises, out of the empty boxes comes a girl, let's hope to tremendous applause.

HOW TO DO IT

As you may have guessed if you've worked it out on a computer, or even if you haven't, you need two boxes for this, one fitting inside the other. They needn't be a very good fit as long as the inner box takes up most of the space in the outer box. The outer box has nothing done to it at all. The inner box needs a little preparation.

You will find that the bottom of the box consists of four flaps that fold over and form the bottom. They will be glued or stapled together, and you must remove the staples and carefully pull the flaps apart. If you damage one of the flaps you can repair it by gluing on a piece of cardboard from some other box. If the outer box you are using has the name of somebody's breakfast cereal printed on it, as it may well have, that's fine, but if it doesn't, just print the word CORN-FLAKES in black with a nice big brush on the outer carton. That's all the preparation you need.

To prepare for the magic, lay the large box on its side, the open top facing the audience. Now the girl you are going to produce creeps inside this box, going in backwards, where she kneels, sitting back on her heels and bending her head down. It's surprising what a small space a girl can pack herself into like this, but you do need a nice small, slim girl. Now you place the smaller box just inside the large box. The open front of this box also faces the audience and you have folded shut the flaps at the bottom. The girl is now hidden by the smaller box and both boxes appear to be empty. See Figure 1.

Draw attention to the boxes and rattle a stick in the smaller box to show how empty it is. Now close the lid or flaps of this small box and gently slide it into the big box. As you do this the girl pushes the flaps that form the bottom upwards, where they fold against the sides of the box and she crawls into the inner box as it is slid in. Now tip the two boxes to an upright position. This is where you will need an assistant and you must do it as if the boxes were empty and light. The girl inside should tilt her weight over to help the boxes stand up. Figure 2.

'Nowadays,' you say, 'we get all sorts of fancy gifts offered

2

with packets of breakfast cereal, but I think we have one here that's rather better than a green plastic aeroplane.' Clap your hands and at this signal the girl jumps up, holds out her arms with a lovely smile and you and your assistants help her to jump out of the boxes and bow to enough applause to shake some of the dust off the ceiling.

Jill-in-the-Box

For this you have a single large carton which you show to be absolutely empty.

'You've all heard of a Jack-in-the-box,' you say. 'But nowadays with all these rules about not discriminating against women, we've changed that. Instead we have a Jill-in-the-box and here she is.'

As you say this a girl pops up and jumps out of the box.

HOW TO DO IT

The box must, of course, be big enough to take a girl but you shouldn't have any difficulty in getting one the right size. It will need some preparation.

1

Cardboard lid fastened to flap of box →

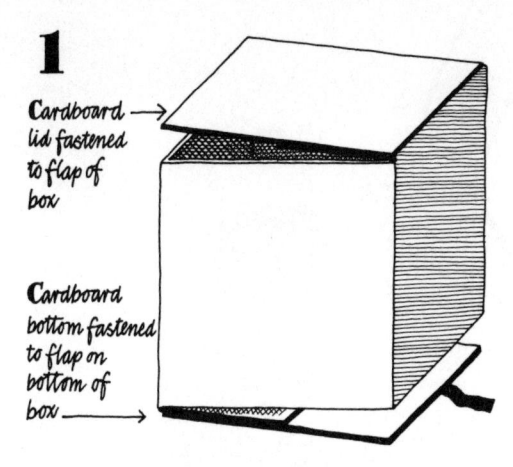

Cardboard bottom fastened to flap on bottom of box →

First cut away all but one of the flaps that close the top of the box. Then, to the remaining flap, glue or staple a piece of cardboard big enough to make a lid for the box. You now have a box with a simple hinged lid.

Next cut away all but one of the flaps that close the bottom of the box. But make sure the flap you leave is the one on the side opposite to that on which the lid is hinged. Figure 1 will make this clear. You now fasten to this flap a piece of cardboard to fill in the bottom. But it must be just small enough to fold up inside the box. See Figure 1 again. To the outside of this hinged bottom you must then fix a little knob or piece of tape.

At the beginning the box stands upright on the floor with the lid closed and the hinged bottom pushed up against the front. The girl is inside, kneeling and squatting back on her heels, and she holds the little knob on the hinged bottom.

To show the box is empty you tilt it forward until it is lying on its front. You can now lift the lid and the box will appear to be empty because the girl is hidden behind it. She holds the hinged lid bottom in place by means of the little knob. Figure 2.

2

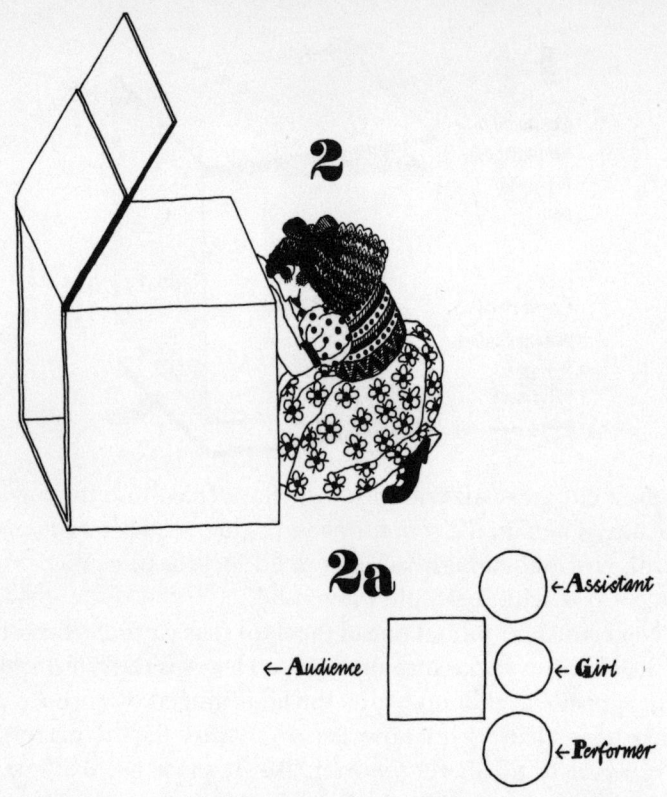

2a ← Assistant
← Audience   ← Girl
← Performer

But, as you may have guessed, people sitting at the sides in the audience would be able to catch a glimpse of the girl behind the box. This is where you need an assistant. He stands on one side of the box and you stand on the other side and tilt the box over between you. You and the assistant thus prevent anyone from seeing round the box and catching sight of the girl. Figure 2a.

Having shown that the box is empty, you and your assistant tilt it back upright again, first closing the lid. Now comes a crafty move that will convince the audience that the box really is empty. You pick it up and turn it completely round, showing the back, then turn it again to bring it back to its original position. This is really quite easy. You just have to be careful to lift the box only a centimetre or so from the floor. In fact you only lift it just enough to slide it round. The girl inside is of course on the floor so you don't have to lift her and she lets go of the knob on the flap and lets the box turn round her. Figure 3.

Finally you announce 'Jill-in-the-box' and the girl pushes up the lid and jumps up. If you have her dressed suitably and made up with round red patches on her cheeks, rather like a Jack-in-the-box, it will make the magic extra-effective.

The Vanishing Lady

Ladies, of course, have a habit of vanishing. You go and look for Mum to ask for more pocket money and you'll find she's vanished. Go into a bank and where the lady who takes the money ought to be there is just a notice saying, 'Till Closed'. The money lady has vanished. There were those useful ladies who used to come in with buckets and mops to help with the housework. They've mostly vanished. And nowadays we get *au pair* girls but they don't come in pairs; there's only one so the other one must have vanished. But here is a way to make a lady vanish just when you want her to.

The lady is, of course, a little girl because little girls pack into smaller boxes than large ladies. The box you make her vanish from is the same one used for Jill-in-the-box. In fact, it is really the same piece of magic in reverse.

You start with the box closed and empty. The bottom flap should be folded up against the front of the box, held in place if necessary with a piece of masking tape. You and your assistant open the lid and help the girl to get into the box. The girl wears a little fancy apron.

You close the lid of the box and say, 'There is a story about the Queen of Incrediblania who complained to a friend that the maid boiled her egg hard. The friend said her maids never stayed long enough for that. And as you see our little maid hasn't stopped long either.'

You and your assistant tip the box over and open the lid. The box is empty because the girl is now behind it as she was at the beginning of the Jill-in-the-box. She has removed the masking tape and pulled the bottom of the box down after her. To make the magic more effective you take out of the box a duplicate of the little apron the girl was wearing. This was hidden in the box behind the folded-up bottom and the front of the box.

'The maid has gone, but she's left her uniform for the next one, if there is one.'

You close the box and tilt it up into an upright position again, which safely hides the girl.

You can now walk forward and do some tricks while your assistant pushes the box off to the side, the girl crawling along inside it.

Quick Change

A girl gets into a box and the lid is closed. A boy picks up a large cloth and slowly raises it to hide him. The cloth is immediately lowered again and the girl is there instead of the boy. The box is then opened and, my word, there is the boy!

The astonishing part of this piece of magic is that the boy simply lifts the cloth up and lowers it again and he is seen to have changed to the girl. The change is quite easy to work but you must rehearse it so that it runs smoothly. Nobody must hurry or they may mess the whole thing up.

HOW TO DO IT

You need a boy and a girl, of course. They should be about the same height but apart from that the less like each other they are the better. They should wear different-coloured clothes but these should be of the close-fitting kind. No flowing draperies to get caught in the works.

The box, which must of course be big enough for the girl or boy to get into, has a piece cut out of the back and hinged

Figure 1: Loop of tape, Turnbutton, Hinged here

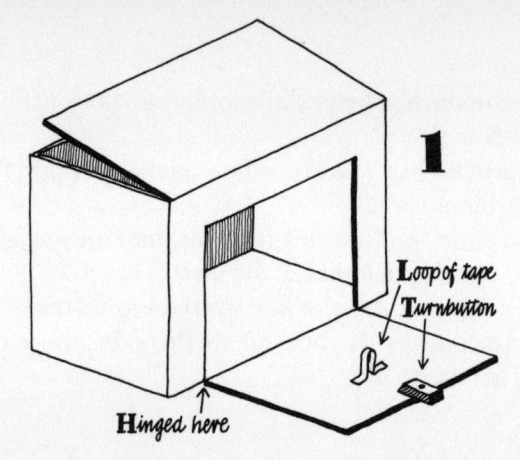

with sticky tape at the bottom. The flap should have a small loop of tape near the top, on the inside, and there should be a turn-button fixed to the inside of the box so that the flap can be held up or dropped down. See Figure 1.

The cloth, which should be a large one – a double blanket would do – must be opaque so as not to let light through. Make a hem along one of the long sides and put a long wooden rod or cane through it.

That's all the apparatus you need.

Now to set it up. The box, with the secret flap in the up position at the back, stands near the back of the stage. Just in front of it and to the left, is the cloth, folded down zig-zag fashion on the floor with the edge with the rod in it on top. One end of the folded cloth should come across a little way in front of the box, as in Figure 2.

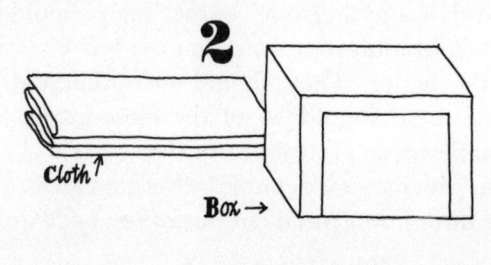

Figure 2: Cloth, Box →

90

To present the magic, introduce the girl, open the box and help her to step in. She crouches down and, as soon as the lid is closed, she opens the flap at the back, lets it drop and crawls out, hiding behind the box. Your assistant is standing on the far side of the box so that the audience at that side cannot catch a glimpse of her and you stand the other side. Now the boy comes on. He stands behind the folded cloth, bends down and picks it up by the centre.

He must hold the cloth in a particular way, with his fingers under the rod and his hands hidden behind the cloth, as shown in Figure 3.

How the boy holds the cloth

He now slowly lifts the cloth. As soon as he has raised it waist high you step away from the box and go to one side. The girl crawls out from behind the box and, hidden by the cloth, crawls along on the left side of the boy. Figure 4. As he continues to raise the cloth she stands up, slides her hands up and takes the cloth from him, holding it in the same way as he did so that her hands are hidden. She continues to raise the cloth and, as soon as it reaches above the boy's head, he drops down and quickly crawls behind the box, gets inside, pulls up the flap and fastens it with the turn-button.

The girl, meantime, without pausing lowers the cloth and reveals herself in place of the boy. She finally drops the cloth to the floor and steps aside. Then you come forward and open the box, and out pops the boy.

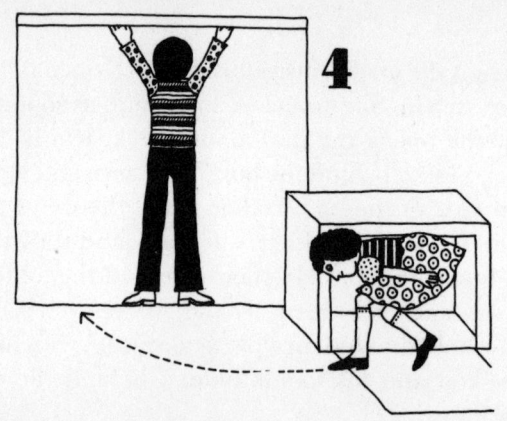

From the front this looks like a remarkable piece of magic. The surprise of the audience, as the girl lowers the cloth and they see her in place of the boy who was there a moment before, is tremendous. Rehearse this piece of magic carefully so that you can go through it smoothly and quickly but without hurry, and you should get a lot of applause. This is a fine piece of magic to close a show.

In this, as in the other magic with people, make sure there is no light shining or reflected from the back because this could reveal the cracks in the box where the secret flap fits.

The Haunted Tower

This is a simplified version of a very puzzling illusion presented many years ago by the master magician David Devant. He called it 'The Vanishing Ghost' and this is what happened.

A number of people were invited up from the audience and formed a large ring round the stage. In the centre of the ring two screens were placed to form an enclosure and into this enclosure went the ghost – someone dressed in white flowing draperies.

A number of other screens were then placed round this centre enclosure so that the ghost was not only trapped inside the two centre screens but was also fenced in by the outer ring of screens and beyond them by the ring of spectators. Yet in spite of all this security, when the screens were removed the ghost had vanished, and he didn't go down a trapdoor because the carpet was first examined by the people from the audience.

Now here is a way to do this piece of people-magic, on the same principle, but without all those screens and without having to get people up from the audience.

The main part of the secret is that the ghost is one of your assistants, dressed exactly the same as the other assistants, but wearing a loose drapery of fine white material that can be rolled up into a small space.

In addition to the ghost you will need four assistants, all dressed alike and, of course, dressed the same as the ghost is dressed under his draperies. And for goodness' sake don't use for your ghost a boy with bright red hair if the others are all dark, or wearing glasses if the others don't.

Apart from the ghost assistant and his drapery, you will need two three-fold screens. That's all.

You begin by saying, 'Let me show you my mysterious haunted tower. It doesn't look much like a tower, nor does it look very mysterious. It is in fact nothing more than two screens. Two very ordinary screens with no trickery about them.'

Your assistants place one of the screens in the centre of the stage with the sides folded forward. They then place the second one in front of the first, with the sides folded backward, so that the two screens form a sort of tower-like enclosure.

'There is the tower,' you say. 'And here comes the ghost who haunts it. Come on, spookie.'

At this point the assistant dressed as the ghost comes on and he should hold his arms out a bit and walk with a sort of gliding movement, in the way ghosts are supposed to walk. Perhaps they get into trouble from the Central Ghost Bureau if they don't.

'Our ghost will now go in and haunt the tower,' you say.

The ghost goes into the space between the screens.

'Haunt away!' you say, and the ghost starts making a wailing noise.

'Ghosts,' you say, 'have a habit of disappearing, and judging by the noise this one is making, the sooner he does it the better. Spookie, kindly vanish!'

The noise stops. Your assistant removes the screens and the ghost has vanished.

HOW TO DO IT

Two assistants come on to remove the screens. Study Figure

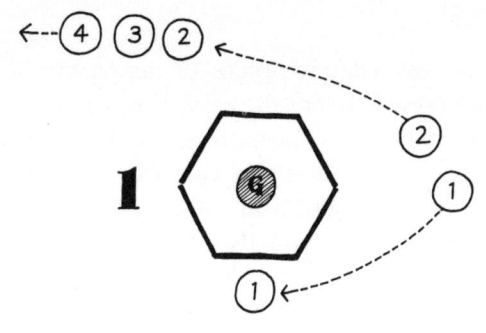

1 and you will see that assistant No. 1 goes to the front screen while assistant No. 2 walks behind the screens and joins two other assistants who are standing at the back of the stage. As the screens are being removed one of these assistants quietly slips off stage into the wings and the other two then come forward and wait to help take the screens away.

Meantime the ghost (G) has taken off his drapery, folded it up small and pushed it up under his jersey or concealed it somewhere else according to what clothes he is wearing. He now looks like one of the assistants.

Assistant No. 1 takes hold of the screen and moves it to the side as shown in Figure 2. As he does this the ghost moves with it and goes round the back of the other screen. Assistant No. 1 now swings the screen round so that the audience can see that the space between the screens is quite empty. The ghost has vanished. And the ghost, now an ordinary assistant, folds up and takes away the other screen. The audience, of course, will take him for assistant No. 2.

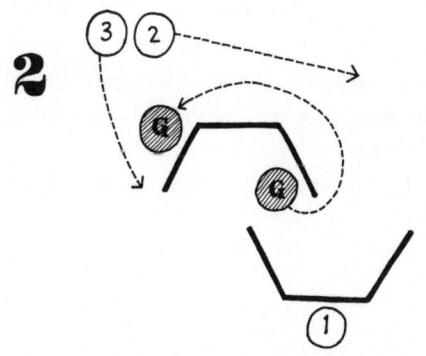

This is a very effective piece of magic but it must be carefully rehearsed so that the assistants know exactly what to do and when to do it. The more assistants you can have on the stage the better but in any case the fact that the ghost becomes an extra assistant will not be noticed because one of the other assistants has quietly gone off stage.

You have also used another device to mislead the audience by drawing attention to the screens, saying they are quite ordinary with no tricks about them. The audience will then suspect that the trick lies in the screens, when of course it doesn't, and so have their attention directed away from the assistants, where the real secret lies.

The Magic Drum

Near the back of your stage is a large cardboard carton with no lid and beside it, leaning against a chair, is another cardboard carton, with no bottom or lid, folded flat.

You show the first carton to be quite empty, put it down, pick up the folded carton, open it out and look through it at the audience so that they can see it also is empty. Your assistant now brings on a large sheet of newspaper and lays it over the first box. You then slide the bottomless box down over the first box, so that the paper forms a sort of drum head, as shown in Figure 1.

'You might think,' you say to the audience, 'that it isn't possible to get much music out of a drum like this. But don't forget the old song "A pretty girl is just like a melody"... Come on, Melody!'

As you say this the paper is burst open and out of the drum comes a girl.

Figure 1: Paper / Inner box / Outer bottomless box

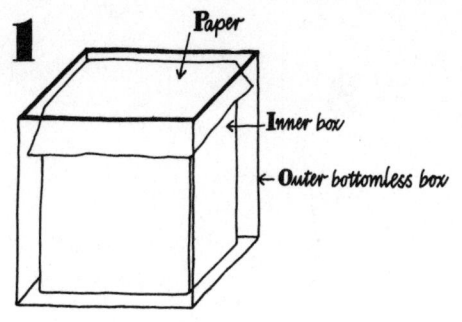

Now if somebody writes in and asks what you do if the girl's name is Sarah I shan't answer.

HOW TO DO IT

The first box you show has the bottom hinged with tape at one side so that it can be pushed up inside the box. You should also fasten a strip of card along the edge of the box opposite to the hinged bottom, so that the bottom can't accidentally drop out. See Figure 2. Both boxes must be tall enough to hide the girl when she is crouched down inside.

To set up for the trick, the girl hides behind the folded box. You pick up the open box and show it is empty, taking care not to let the bottom fall inwards. The best way to do this is to hold the box with the hinged side of the flap at the top.

When you have shown the box, put it down behind the folded box and over the girl. As you do this, you press the hinged bottom upwards and the girl also helps to push up the flap and settle the box over herself. You then pick up the folded box and walk forward, opening it and showing it empty by looking through it at the audience.

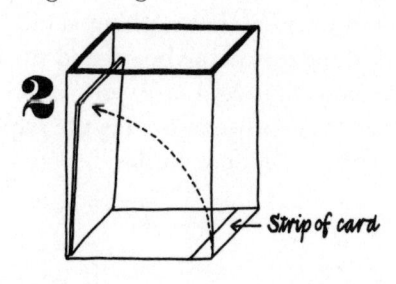

Figure 2: Strip of card

3

← Chair

← Girl hidden
behind folded box

← Folded bottomless box

← Box with hinged bottom

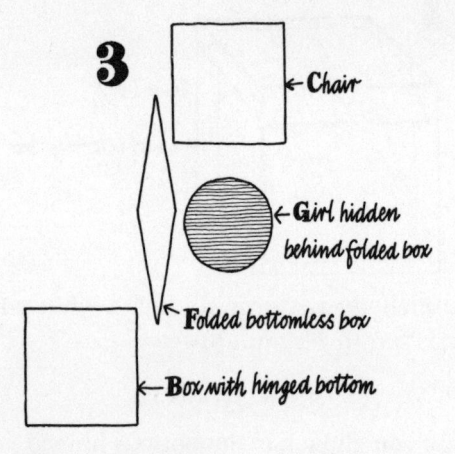

View looking down

This is the crucial movement in the trick. To the audience you appear to have put the box down and picked up the folded one. You must rehearse it so that you can drop the box down casually over the girl and almost with the same movement pick up the folded box. The audience, of course, having seen that the box has a solid bottom, won't suspect that you are putting it down over anything, but you mustn't do it clumsily or they'll think something secret is being done.

Your assistant now brings on the paper. This can be two double sheets of newspaper stuck together to form one large sheet. The assistant lays it over the box with the girl in it and you then slide the bottomless box down over it, making a sort of drum. See Figure 1.

You and your assistant can then slide the drum forward and turn it round to show that nothing is hidden behind it. The girl crawls along inside the boxes and the audience will get the impression that you are just moving two light cardboard boxes. The girl then breaks the paper and jumps up in the box with a ten-acre smile.

98

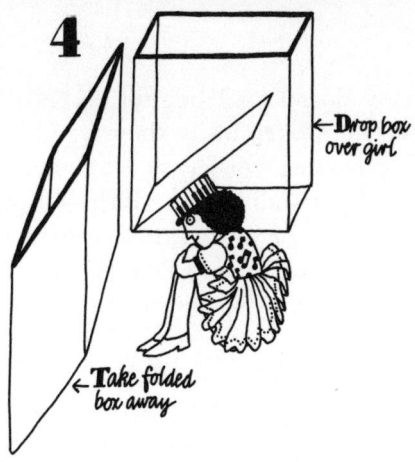

You might like to make the magic even more effective by having the girl dressed in a costume with musical notes painted on it and perhaps a head-dress made to look like a piano keyboard.

Sorcerer's Swiss Roll

Two assistants bring on a large piece of corrugated cardboard. It is about 1½ m high and 3 m long. Your teacher will be able to get corrugated cardboard of this size from a firm that makes packing materials. You want the kind that can be rolled up, not the rigid sort. If you can't get corrugated cardboard big enough, you can use a large cloth, made by sewing two old blankets together, or any other material that is opaque.

Your assistants hold the cloth or cardboard upright, and then the assistant holding the right-hand end moves across in front of the other and walks right round, making the cloth into a sort of vertical roll. The assistant at the other end moves back as he does so, still holding his end of the cloth, so that he doesn't get mixed up in the roll.

'What we have done,' you say to the audience, 'is to make a large Swiss roll. Now all we want is the jam and here it is.'

Your assistants lift the roll of cardboard and there inside is a girl. If you are using a cloth they just let the cloth drop down and the girl comes out of the middle of it.

HOW TO DO IT

The method is exactly the same whether you are using a roll of corrugated cardboard or a large cloth. But if you use a cloth your assistants must hold it by the top edge with their hands as far apart as possible, to hold the cloth up.

I will assume you are using a cloth.

When your assistants bring on the cloth, the girl walks on behind it. She must of course be small enough not to be seen over the top of the cloth. The assistants must be a good bit taller than the girl and they must let the cloth touch the floor as they come in so that the girl's feet can't be seen beneath it.

Now follow the diagrams and you'll see how she gets into the cloth as it is rolled round.

Figure 1 shows the cloth as it is brought on. G is the girl and the assistants are numbered 1 and 2.

In Figure 2, assistant No. 1 is walking round with the cloth, in front of assistant No. 2. As soon as he has passed assistant No. 2, thus hiding the other edge of the cloth, the girl runs round and into the cloth, as in Figure 3. Assistant No. 1 continues to walk round, making the cloth into a vertical roll and assistant No. 2 moves back, still holding the cloth, so that between them they can complete the roll with the girl inside.

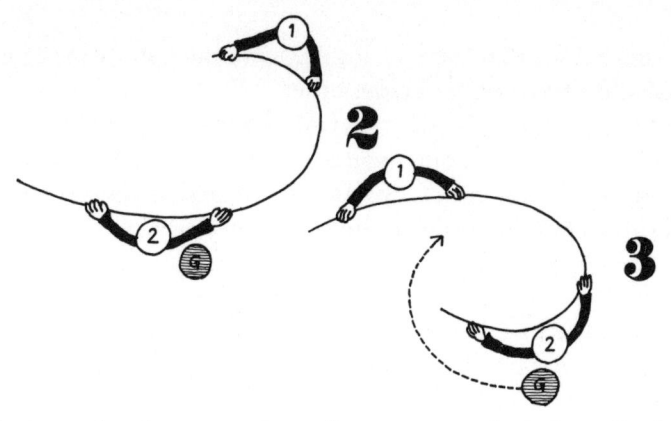

The whole business is easier with a sheet of flexible corrugated cardboard, but it can be done with a cloth. If you find it difficult to hold the cloth up, make a hem along the top of it and insert a long piece of fairly thick cardboard into the hem. This will give you a firm edge to get hold of. Leave the ends of the hem open so that you can renew the cardboard if it gets too soft and crumpled with use.

It is a good idea, when presenting magic of this kind, to have suitable music playing while the preparations are being made. A march tune is appropriate, and someone in the wings can do it with a record, or play it on a piano.

Down the Chimney

You have three large cardboard tubes, one red, one yellow and one blue. 'These,' you explain, 'are three chimneys which we bought from a fiddler on the roof.' You hold each one up in turn so that the audience can see right through them and see that there is nothing concealed in them. Then you slide them one over the other.

'You may wonder why we want chimneys, with all these smokeless zones about,' you say. 'Well, the reason is that Santa Claus doesn't much care about coming down a chimney that isn't there and landing on an electric fire. So we have to use chimneys for him to come down, and here he is!'

As you say this you and one of your assistants lift up all three tubes together and there is Santa Claus, or at least a little girl or boy dressed as Santa Claus.

HOW TO DO IT

You want four tubes (not three). They must all be of different widths so that they can fit easily over one another.

The smallest tube must be big enough for the little girl who is going to play Santa, to stand inside, and tall enough to come above her head. This tube is painted dead black. The others are painted respectively yellow, red and blue.

The tubes can be made of very wide, flexible, corrugated cardboard, the same kind as you used for the 'Swiss roll'. Or they can be made from sheets of thin cardboard fastened together with push-through-bend-over paper fasteners. If you use these fasteners, always put a bit of sticky tape over the folded-down points so that they won't catch anybody. If you can choose a really little girl for this piece of magic your tubes needn't be much more than a metre high. The other tubes must be several centimetres taller than this tube.

To set up for the magic, slide the smallest, black tube over the little girl as she stands on the stage. As the top of the tube is open she won't stifle.

Place the other three tubes in a triangle in front of the black one, as shown in Figure 1. The yellow tube is at the front, the blue one to the left and the red one to the right.

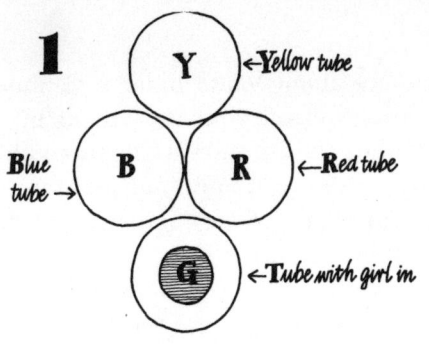

1 — Yellow tube ← Y
Blue tube → B   R ← Red tube
G ← Tube with girl in

These three tubes hide the tube with the girl in it from the audience.

Now to show the tubes empty. First you pick up the yellow tube, let the audience see through it, then put it down over the hidden tube with the girl inside it. You hold the tube up high above your head to let the audience see through it, and it will look quite natural for you to turn it upright and lower it secretly over the hidden tube.

Without pausing you immediately pick up the red tube, show it and slide it over the yellow tube. Then you show the blue tube and slide that down over the others. The tubes are now all nested with Santa inside as in Figure 2.

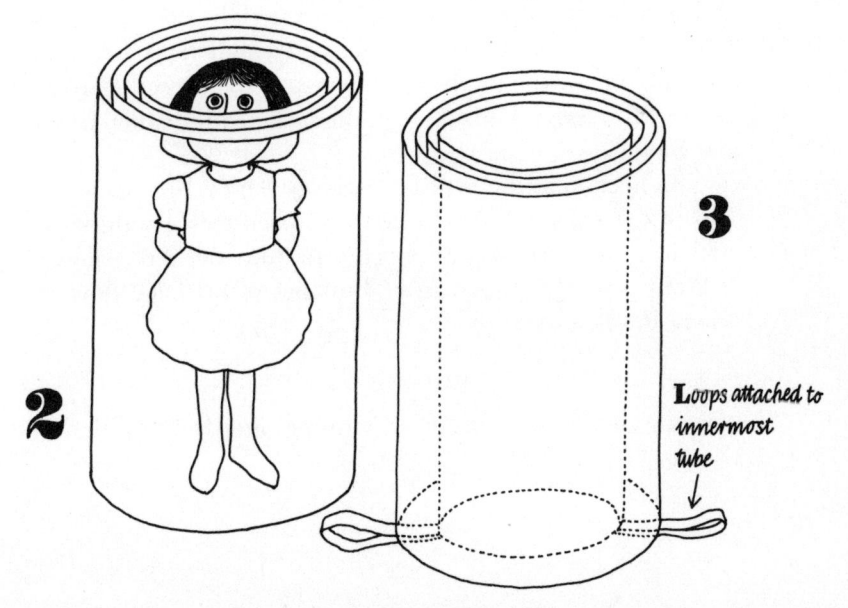

2

3 Loops attached to innermost tube ↓

Say your piece about Santa liking a chimney or two to come down. Then you and your assistant lift up all four tubes together, revealing the little girl. To do this without exposing the secret inner tube, you and your assistant should bend down and get the fingers of one hand under the tubes and lift, while you support the tubes with the other hand.

You can make this lifting business easier if you fix two short loops of thick string to the bottom of the secret tube, one at each side. You and your assistant can then lift all the tubes quite easily by simply holding the string loops. See Figure 3.

Presents from Santa Claus

In the last piece of magic you produced a little Santa Claus. Wouldn't it be nice if your Santa Claus now produced presents for the audience? Right.

You show a large red sack and turn it inside out to show that it is quite empty. You then turn it right side out again and say, 'This is the sack Santa carries all the Christmas presents in. At the moment, as you see, the presents are all absent. But Santa finds them in the sack just the same. Come on, Santa.'

You beckon to the little girl playing Santa. She opens the top of the sack, reaches inside and produces a number of articles. These can be presents for the audience if the show is a family one. Or they can be bunches of artificial flowers, fancy boxes and so on.

HOW TO DO IT

Santa's sack is an extremely cunning one. It has a double

bottom, as shown in Figure 1. To make it you need a shallow circular container. The bigger the container the more things you can produce from it. The container can be a large round tin of the kind fancy biscuits are sold in, or you can make the container from cardboard, in which case you can make it as big as you like. The top of the container is cut across the centre and one half is hinged to open like a lid. If you use a tin for the container you must make the top of cardboard so as to hinge it with tape.

The bag is made from any kind of red material and is simply a strip of material wide enough to go round the container with an overlap of a few centimetres. Stick the material to the sides of the container, folding the edges under and sticking them down. Cover the top of the container with the same material or paint it to match, and sew the sides of the sack together. Figure 1.

Fill the container with whatever articles you want Santa to produce.

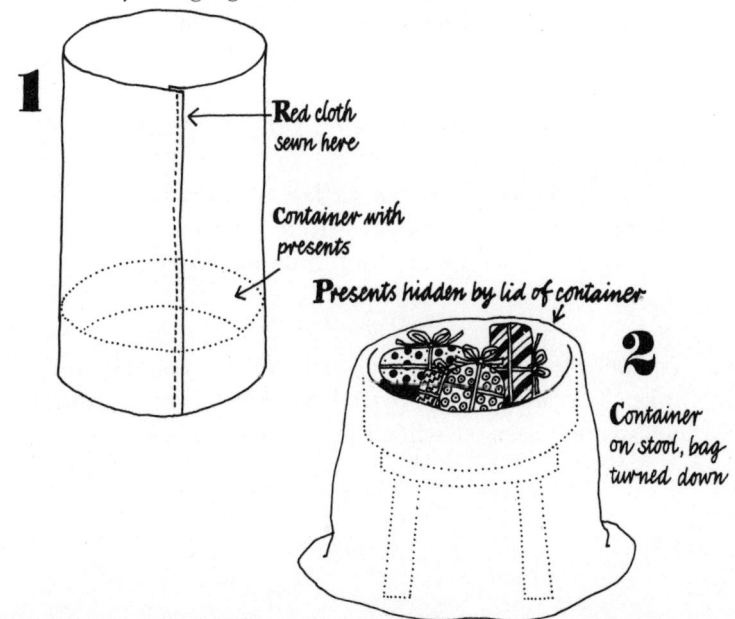

Bring on the sack and stand it on a low stool. Turn the sack inside out by bringing the mouth of the sack down and round the bottom as shown in Figure 2. The bag appears to be empty because what the audience take to be the bottom of the sack is really the top of the container. You must put the sack on a low stool otherwise the audience may notice that the bottom of the bag is too high up.

Now draw the mouth of the bag up again and let Santa Claus produce the presents. All she has to do is reach inside the bag, open the half lid and take out the articles. It's as easy as falling off a yule log.

The Great Escape Act

You have a very large paper bag, big enough to hold your girl assistant. You can make this by pasting sheets of newspaper together. Having shown the bag, you open it out and stand it in a large, deep carton. Your assistant now gets into the bag. To do this she will need to stand on a chair and step down into the bag, helped by you and your assistants.

She crouches down inside the bag and you tie the mouth of the bag firmly with string or ribbon and close the lid of the box.

'That's one way to bag a girl,' you say. 'Safely tied up and can't get out.'

As you say this the lid of the box opens and the girl jumps out, holding the paper bag, still tied. You untie it and show that the bag is complete and undamaged.

HOW TO DO IT

You need two paper bags, both made of newspaper and both alike. You needn't go to the trouble of getting duplicate newspapers because when the bags are made up nobody will be able to remember exactly what each bag looks like. Of course the audience do not know that there are two bags.

You also need a large, deep cardboard carton with a hinged lid. This must be big enough for the girl to crouch down in and still have some room to move.

To prepare, take one of the newspaper bags and tie the mouth with string. Fold it loosely and lay it in the bottom of the box, to one side. That's all.

To perform, show the other bag, letting the audience see that it is a complete bag, with no holes anywhere except the one at the top where you put things in. Open out the bag and stand it in the box. You and your assistants now help the girl in. She crouches down in the bag and you tie the mouth of it over her head.

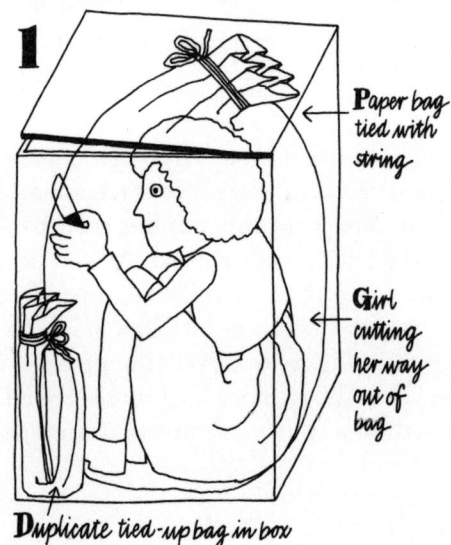

While you are doing this, the girl secretly cuts the bag open down the front with a penknife which she has concealed in her hand. Figure 1. She does this as quietly as possible and it will help if you have some fairly loud music playing while you tie up the bag and close the box. This will seem quite natural to the audience as there is nothing for you to say during the tying-up period and the music keeps the interest going.

You close the box. The girl immediately pulls the top of the bag down round her, presses the bag down in the bottom of the box, picks up the duplicate bag and jumps up. You help her out of the box, untie the bag she is holding and show that it is still complete and undamaged. While you are doing this, your assistants close the box and push it off into the wings.

ANOTHER WAY OF DOING IT

For this you don't use paper bags, but bags made of some thin material. Both bags must be exactly alike. One of them is folded up small with just the top free, as shown in Figure 2.

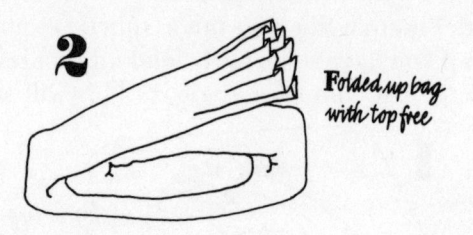

Folded up bag with top free

Your girl assistant has this bag concealed under her jumper. You show the other bag, place it in the box and help the girl to climb into it. Now you gather up the mouth of the bag and proceed to tie it with a wide ribbon. As you do this, the girl takes the folded bag from under her jumper and pushes the top of it up through the visible bag. You hold the tops of both bags as shown in Figure 3 and tie the piece of wide ribbon round them. The ribbon hides the join between the bags and the audience think you have simply tied up the bag with the girl in it.

3

Wide ribbon

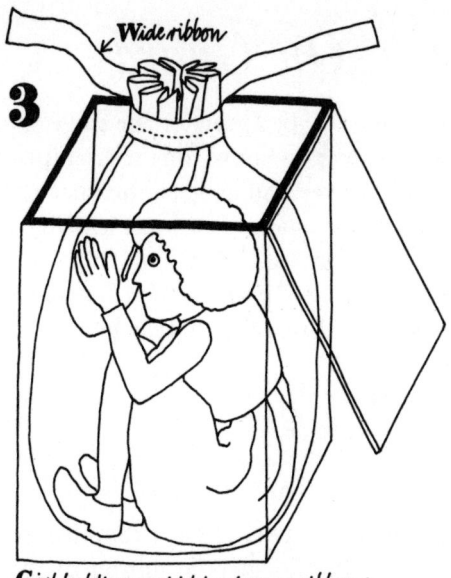

Girl holding up hidden bag as ribbon is tied round both bags

You now take an ordinary luggage label and tie it to the ribbon. Then you ask someone in the audience to come up and write his name on the label.

The girl crouches down in the box and you close the lid. She immediately pulls the mouth of the bag down round her. She steps out of it and out of the box, holding the duplicate bag, which she first unfolds. You ask the person who wrote his name on the label to verify that it is the same label, and therefore, it seems, it must be the same bag.

Of course, you don't have to use a cardboard carton for this. Whichever method you use any large box or hamper or trunk that you happen to have will do, as long as there is plenty of room in it for the girl.

On Guard

You have a long narrow box lying on the stage. You and your assistants turn it over to show that it is empty. Then you continue turning it over and over on the floor until the open side comes uppermost again. You cover it with a large Union Jack and stand the box upright.

'This, as you can see,' you say, 'is a sort of sentry box without any sentry. But he's there when he's wanted ... Turn out the Guard!'

As you say this the flag is twitched aside and out steps a girl, dressed as a soldier.

HOW TO DO IT

The box must be about 30 cm longer than the girl is high, so once again the smaller the girl the shorter the box. One way to make the box is to use a number of boxes, cut the ends out of some of them, and join them all together in one long box. Or you can make it by sticking or stapling several sheets of cardboard together, then bending up the sides and ends as shown in Figures 1 and 2. Apart from being longer than the girl, the box needs to be big enough for her to lie in comfortably, not a tight fit.

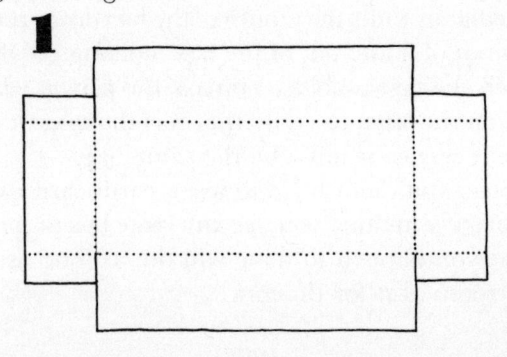

1

2 How the long box is made

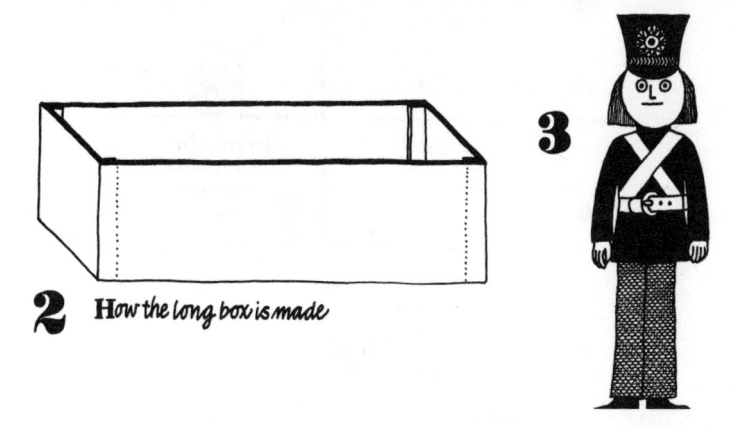

3

To make it look more like a sentry box you can, if you like, bend up a triangle of cardboard and fasten it on top of the box.

The girl can be dressed as a soldier quite simply, with blue trousers and a red jumper and a cardboard hat. Criss-cross strips of white material and a white belt as shown in Figure 3 will also help.

The box lies on the floor with the open side uppermost and the long side facing the audience. The girl lies behind the box. Your assistants take the box, one at each end and tip it over to show it is empty. As they do this the girl rolls over, keeping close against the box. Your assistants now turn the box again and again. The girl rolls along behind the box, and, as soon as the open side of the box comes to the back, she rolls inside. Figure 4.

Your assistants turn the box open side up and spread the flag over it. If you can't get a big enough flag you can use any piece of material, but your school will almost certainly have a Union Jack you can get them to lend you. Clip the flag to the

4

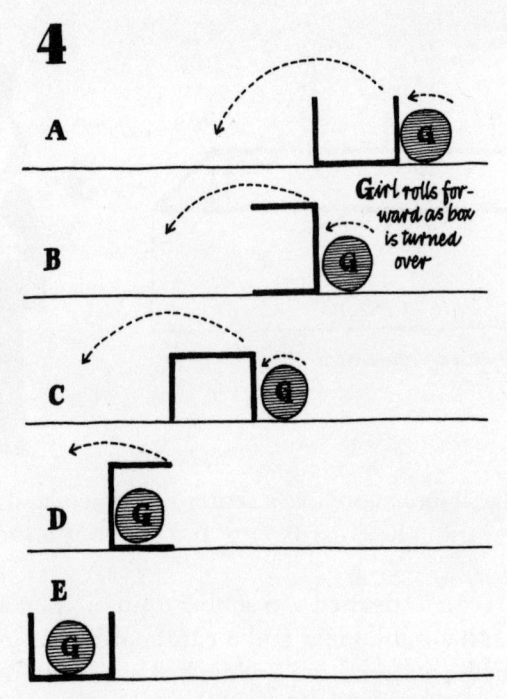

A

B Girl rolls forward as box is turned over

C

D

E

top end of the box with a couple of clothes pegs so that it won't fall off when you stand the box up.

Now lift one end of the box. And do make sure you lift the end where the girl's head is. Stand the box on end with the open, flag-covered side facing the audience. Do this standing-up of the box gently or otherwise the poor girl will be shot out and you'll get a huge laugh from the audience, but not the kind of laugh you want.

Now with the box safely upright and covered with the flag you shout, 'Turn out the Guard!' and the girl pulls the flag aside, steps out and salutes. If the audience don't applaud that, shoot them with the nearest pop-gun.

Professor Flittersnoop
and Mrs Branestawm

This piece of magic is a simplified, and adapted version of an illusion devised a long time ago by a celebrated American magician, U. F. Grant.

The magician has on the stage with him a boy and a girl. He gives the boy some clothes to dress up as Professor Branestawm. Then he gives the girl clothes to dress up as Mrs Flittersnoop.

The boy and girl stand one on each side of the stage.

'Now,' says the magician, 'I want you to change places.' And the Professor and Mrs Flittersnoop each walk across the stage to opposite sides.

'Oh, that's a dull way of changing places,' says the magician. 'Do it by magic.' He claps his hands. Professor Branestawm takes off his disguise and the audience see that he is really the girl. Mrs Flittersnoop does the same and turns out to be the boy.

This is a real wowzie, if you'll pardon the Incrediblanian expression, especially to finish a show.

HOW TO DO IT

You will need, of course, a boy and a girl. They should be the same size and height. You will also need a second boy. He must be the same size and height as the other two and he should wear the same kind of trousers and shoes as the other boy. He should also, if possible, have the same colour and style of hair. The audience do not know of the existence of this second boy and he is behind the screen or off stage at the start of the trick.

You bring on the other boy and the girl and you say you are going to get them to dress up as Professor Branestawm and Mrs Flittersnoop. You give the boy clothes for the Professor. These consist of a long, loose-fitting grey coat. The kind of overall coat that painters and warehousemen wear is ideal and can be bought at shops that sell overalls and boiler suits. The coat should be long enough to reach right to the ground and be rather too big for the boy. Then you will need a comic mask, which you can buy at a novelty shop. This mask should have a pair of spectacles on it. If it hasn't you can make a pair from cardboard and stick them on. You will also need a large felt hat that will come down well over the boy's ears and hide his hair.

The boy takes these things and goes behind the screen. But he doesn't put them on. Instead the second boy puts them on and comes out on to the stage.

To cover the time the boy will take to put the clothes on you explain that the Professor takes a little time to dress and that you mustn't hurry him or otherwise he may put his clothes on upside-down or inside-out.

When the second boy, dressed as the Professor, comes out, he stands on the side of the stage. You then give to the girl some clothes for her to dress up as Mrs Flittersnoop. These consist of a long, loose overall, buttoning down the front. It should reach right to the ground and be a bit too large for the girl, just as the Professor's coat was too large for the boy. The overall for Mrs Flittersnoop should be a bright colour and, if possible, of flowered material. You also give her a suitable mask and a large floppy hat that will hide her hair. The girl, by the way, has to have short hair.

The girl takes the clothes and goes behind the screen. But she doesn't put the Mrs Flittersnoop clothes on. Instead the boy, the one the audience saw to start with and who is waiting there, puts on the Mrs Flittersnoop clothes. He comes out and stands on the other side of the stage.

And just as you made up the time to allow the Professor to dress, you explain to the audience that ladies always take a bit of time to dress, and you can't hurry ladies or otherwise they forget to draw their eyebrows straight or leave something behind.

You now have the boy the audience have seen, dressed as Mrs Flittersnoop, and you have the second boy (whom the audience haven't seen) dressed as the Professor. Behind the screen the girl has put on a duplicate coat and mask of the Professor. She also has in her hand four pairs of spectacles, dummy ones, of course, or toy ones. She waits there unseen.

You now look at the boy dressed as Professor Branestawm and say, 'My dear Professor, you're so absent-minded. But then we all know you are, and you've forgotten some of your spectacles. You've got only one pair and you should have five. Please go and get the other pairs as we want you all complete.'

The boy dressed as the Professor unbuttons the lower part of his coat and feels in his trousers' pocket, then waves his hand and says, 'Oh dear, yes, tut, tut. How careless of me! Excuse me while I get the other pairs.' He goes behind the screen. The girl, dressed as the Professor, puts on the boy's Professor hat and comes on waving the four pairs of spectacles.

You now have the two children the audience saw to begin with, dressed as Mrs Flittersnoop and the Professor. But of course it is the girl who is dressed as the Professor and the boy who is dressed as Mrs Flittersnoop.

You then ask the children to change places and they cross over to opposite sides of the stage. When you say, 'Let's do it by magic', you clap your hands and the children take off the disguises showing that Mrs Flittersnoop is the boy and the Professor is the girl.

The important thing here is that right up to the last minute, the audience are allowed to see that the person in the Professor Branestawm disguise is a boy and they naturally assume it is the boy they first saw, as they don't know what is going to happen. It seems quite a natural bit of fun to make the Professor forget his spectacles and as he simply goes behind the screen and immediately comes back the audience have no idea that it is really the girl disguised as the Professor who comes out with the spectacles.

To make everything quite clear let me sum up what happens.
1 Boy and girl on stage in front of audience.
2 Second boy behind screen. Also behind screen

second Professor coat, mask, and four pairs of spectacles.
3 Boy on stage goes behind screen with Professor disguise but other boy puts it on and comes out.
4 Girl on stage goes behind screen with Mrs Flittersnoop disguise but boy who is there puts it on and comes on stage.
5 Girl behind screen puts on second Professor coat and mask and picks up the four pairs of spectacles.
6 Boy on stage dressed as Professor goes behind screen to fetch spectacles. But girl takes off his hat, puts it on and goes on stage carrying the four pairs of spectacles.
7 Boy on stage is now dressed as Mrs Flittersnoop and girl on stage is dressed as the Professor.
8 They cross over and change places.
9 They remove their disguises and show that the one dressed as Mrs Flittersnoop is now the boy and the one dressed as the Professor is the girl.

You may find it helpful to have someone behind the screen to help your actors put the clothes on. But they obviously have to have time to dress, and you, the magician, explain that to the audience.

Rehearse this piece of magic carefully so that it can be done calmly without hurry and you'll find it will produce gasps of astonishment from the audience as the Professor and Mrs Flittersnoop apparently magically change places.

One final word. Don't describe this piece of magic on your programme as 'Professor Flittersnoop and Mrs Branestawm' because that might give the audience a clue as to what is going to happen. Simply call it 'Professor Branestawm and Mrs Flittersnoop'.